M000211318

HUPERMAN

TRANSFORMING TO A LIFE BEYOND LIMITS

DUANE WHITE

DREAM
TREE
PRESS

You hold in your hands a book replete with enormously valuable truth and insights. The revelations in *Huperman* could mark the pivotal point of your life. Over the years, I've been privileged to endorse a good number of fine books. But never—until now—have I said that, after reading this book, everything in your life can be greater. Pastor Duane White unveils a life-expanding open secret. While it is always good to pray, "Lord, what is your will for my life?", it is far more consequential to pray, "Lord, what is your will for my generation, and how do you want to use my life to fulfill your plans for my times?" *Huperman* doesn't give you next steps; it invites you into a new dimension of enabling grace and fulfillment.

–**Dr. David Shibley, Founder, Global Advance**

When Duane White first shared his idea of "Huperman," I thought it was a joke. But once I started to explore the meaning and history of the word, it didn't take long for me to realize just how powerful it is. His new updated book, *Huperman: Transforming to a Life Beyond Limits,* is an unusual take on a transformational concept. Get the book. Because everyone has a boundary they need to break through, or a ceiling they need to shatter.

–**Phil Cooke, Ph.D., Media producer, consultant, and author of *The Way Back: How Christians Blew Our Credibility And How We Get It Back***

Pastor Duane unleashed so many truths in this book! Christ in us makes us invincible. We can all be HUPERMAN by God's HUPER anointing! Such an engaging read from start to finish. We felt Holy Spirit radiating from the pages. If you want to change your mindset and allow the Holy Spirit to unleash *huper* power in your life READ THIS BOOK! It is perfect for any season of your life. We recommend this read once a year!

–Carlos and Alexa PenaVega, Actor/Actress & Media Influencers

I've learned that revisiting turning points in our lives helps to remind us of where we've been and where we're going. My friend Duane has done that with this book. The updates and expansions don't *rehash* what was, they *refresh* the truth of what is! Prepare to be encouraged, inspired, and empowered.

–Tim Ross, Lead Pastor, Embassy City Church, Irving, Texas

Duane's story has inspired me and many around the world and will inspire you. The *huper* principles shared are must-know practical advice that will help you break through barriers and launch you into the MORE God has for you.

–Louis Kotze, Sr. Pastor, Hatfield Christian Church, Pretoria, South Africa

It's been said, "If you can change what you believe, you can change your life." I couldn't agree more. Are there lies about your new spiritual identity that you're believing? In his book, *Huperman*, Duane White, teaches in a very practical, yet powerful way how to break the power of those lies. My dear friend, Duane White, isn't just putting the effort into speaking this message, but rather he has spent a lifetime living it. If you're ready to break free from the hold of the devil's lies and begin to see who you truly are in Christ, this book is truth that will set you free! WARNING: After reading *Huperman* you just might enjoy life more!

–Ben Dailey, Sr. Pastor. Calvary Church, Dallas, Texas, Author of *Limitless* and *Collide*, overseer of Gospel Circle of Churches and Ministries

Real. Relevant. Duane interweaves biblical truths with personal stories to help you declare the TRUTH of God's Word over your "seen realities" and live a "Huperman" life.

–Mike Kai, Sr. Pastor, Inspire Church, Honolulu, Hawaii

Duane White has not only produced a book—he has LIVED a LIFE! As both ministry colleagues and friends, it has been our privilege to watch the truths presented in *Huperman* take shape, not only in preaching, but just as importantly, in LIVING! As you read these pages, you will sense the Holy Spirit making Scripture even more real to you, but you will also receive an impartation of faith from Duane's lifestyle of overcoming! This book falls in the all too narrow category of transformational reading that not only stirs the heart and shapes the thinking, but also provides a clear role model for victorious Kingdom living! We are thrilled to recommend it to one and all!

–Paul and Perrianne Brownback, Sr. Pastors of The Abbey Church, Ft. Worth, Texas

Duane has a remarkable story of what God has done in and through him, a story that has impacted many around the world. Having known Duane as a friend and as someone who has faithfully minis-tered to our church over many years, I can testify that he is a great model of the "huper" life that this book so clearly portrays. Read and be inspired!

–Dr. Dave Smith, Sr. Pastor, KingsGate Community Church, UK

I love a 2000-year-old scripture that says "… in all these things we are more than conquerors…" (Romans 8:37). I like to tell people that in the Greek language of the day "more than conquerors" is "Huper Nike" which is not too far from the truth (hypernikomen). This means we are not just getting through our circumstances, but we are coming through better, stronger, bolder, with more freedom, joy and peace.

"More than" is Duane's life, "more than" is Duane's message, "more than" is actually Duane White himself. If anyone can help you into the MORE that God has for you, I believe that Duane, whom I'm pleased to call my friend, can. I am certain you do not have this book by accident. God desires through this message to guide you into the more He has for you. Therefore, I encourage you, read this book with faith, read with expectation because there is so much more coming your way. You are "more than" a conqueror!

–Paul Benger, Lead Pastor, IKON Church, UK

Some people are hard to 'read'. The Apostle Paul writing about his friends in the church at Corinth writes, 'Your very lives are a letter that anyone can read by just looking at you.' Reading my friend Duane White's latest book gives people an opportunity to read not only the book but also the man.

–Stuart Bell, Leader of Ground Level Network, Sr. Pastor of Alive Church, UK

What makes this book deeply compelling and spiritually powerful is how the truths Duane shares were discovered on a lifelong journey. It is rooted in scripture, outworked in real life. *Huperman* is faith-filled, hope-giving and yet powerfully practical. I wholeheartedly recommend this compelling read, it really does have the potential to thrust you into a new dimension of living!

–Steve Uppal, Senior Leader, All Nations Church, Wolver-hampton, UK

What a strategic season for the release of this revised edition of *Huperman*. Our society bathes us in a culture which conditions people to manage their own human potential. The mantra is "you can have it all." Secular media tells them, "You are entitled to your dream." This formulates a new version of the Superman myth that unlimited possibilities live within mere human potential, yet it yields disillusionment. In *Huperman*, Duane White explains a deeper truth. God unlocks our divine potential deposited in each one of us. God's dream for us realized in our lives! Duane leads us on a path of trading strife for what is merely *SUPER* to finding God's great, fulfilling grace in what is *HUPER*. *Hupermen* (and women) neither disappoint nor are they disappointed!

–Jack Groblewski, Sr. Pastor, New Covenant Christian Community, Bethlehem, PA

Many preachers say many things, but if you search a little deeper with a true Father or Mother in the faith, you'll often find something more than mere information or good principles. In all the Greats there runs a vein of divine glory gold that is their life message. These messages pulsate with more life than mere teaching. They impart and carry an unusual grace, almost as if it was living and breathing in a heavenly way that exceeds basic good teaching. *Huperman* is one of those messages—a living vein of gold, ready to impart Jesus and transform hearts with a fresh upgrade of God's love, faith and grace. I love Duane White. I love the heavenly deposit within these teachings—Duane's life-message. What you hold is not a mere book, but another gateway where heaven has touched earth! Be ready for transformation as you read & meditate upon its contents—you may never be the same again!

–Jarrod Cooper, Senior Leader, Revive Church; Founder of The Tribe, UK

CONTENTS

FOREWORD

As I got into the car to return to my hotel, my mind filled with curiosity over what the last few hours could have given 'birth' to. Not just for my life personally, but for the life of the young man I had just met. For over three hours at the 'elegant' Denny's restaurant he asked questions and shared dreams that were glimpses of a God-designed destiny for his life and, ultimately, mine as well. That night a deep and lifelong friendship with Duane White was born that has taken us to faraway places, amazing events, days and nights of laughter, and even difficult and painful moments.

In hindsight, looking back on that night over twenty-five years ago, the insights and inspirational truths you are holding in your hand as a book were emerging realities in his life even then. *Huperman: Transforming to a Life Beyond Limits* is powerful because it not only invites us to examine a theory, but welcomes us on the journey that has become a way of life for Duane.

Far too often we are all tempted to allow our perceived deficiencies and visible flaws to lull us into self-imposed limitations that paralyze our pursuit of purpose and dreams. We slumber through moments of opportunity, more consumed by 'who we are not' than coming to grips with 'who we really are'! Through the stories and principles of this book I am positive that an alarm clock will sound and your 'wake up' call will arrive.

As Duane reveals his own journey in overcoming obstacles to pages meant to unveil the good news of the gospel that liberates the soul from excuses, *Huperman* is a roadmap for discovering God's amazing grace. You are far more than you think you are! In a culture that prizes success, we struggle to find the proper metrics by which to measure it. But through the insights in this book you will learn that one cannot define success through wealth or earthly things we accumulate. The 'why' of our life is not answered by notoriety, education or status, but when we refuse to live hesitantly and step into the 'exceeding' life God ordained for us to live. Abundant, super-sized living—that is where success is realized!

I trust this book will not be a casual read for you, but rather a guidebook you reference often. I hope it marks your life, just as it has my friend Duane and so many of us, causing you to live your life "beyond" the boundaries that our culture has determined disqualify you or marginalize you. After all, you too are a part of that 'holy nation' of Hupermen and Huperwomen!

Bishop Tony Miller (tonymiller.tv)
Author of *Journey to Significance*, Sr. Pastor of The Gate Church in Oklahoma City, OK, Leader of the Destiny Fellowship of Churches and Ministries

INTRODUCTION

Don't You Mean Superman?

HUPER, in Greek, means "beyond, over, more than, exceedingly." This is exciting because God takes our average, ordinary lives and adds His HUPER strength to break through our limits. Just as it says in Ephesians 3:20, God *"is able to do exceedingly abundantly above all that we ask or think. . . . "*

Could you use some HUPER strength to overcome the limits you're facing?

Several years ago, I had a short stopover in England on my way to conduct a pastors' conference in India. My friends asked if I would minister to their church in the seaport town of Grimsby. This struggling city was the perfect backdrop for God to download His *huper* revelation to me. Known as "Great Grimsby," it once supported the largest fishing fleet in the world, but had battled a postindustrial decline, shifting it from "great" to "grim." My text that evening was 2 Corinthians 4:7, *"But we have this treasure in earthen vessels, that the excellency of the power may be of God and not of us."* I explained how the word "excellency" is from the Greek *huperbole* (like our English word hyperbole). It means "to throw beyond; an exaggeration," and the prefix, huper, takes something beyond itself to an exceeding abundance.

That night in front of an eclectic but eager crowd, I shared my testimony of how God took a timid cleft lip and cleft palate boy who was told he'd never be able to speak and transformed him into an international preacher. It was a wonderful evening. At the conclusion, a sweet elderly lady shuffled up to meet me. In her polite British accent, she asked, "Have you ever heard of the British comedy with the character named Cooperman?" I told her I had not, and she continued, "Well, surely you've heard of Superman, the American superhero?" I assured her that, yes, I had heard of Superman—everyone's heard of Superman!

I must admit, I wondered where this conversation was going or if I was missing something in the British-to-American translation. With a fire in her eyes, she persisted, "As you were preaching, I got a revelation of this 'beyond' life you described. I kept feeling the Lord wants you to know you are not Cooperman nor are you Superman; you are HUPERMAN!" Something leaped in my spirit. It was one of those "aha" moments where you feel you've stepped through to another dimension. God used this unassuming lady to plant a seed of destiny that would change my life.

A few months later, my friend Mike Noviskie traveled with me to Kenya and heard me preach the "Huperman" message. A few weeks after our return home, our paths crossed again, and he presented me with a special gift. We laughed as I held up the white T-shirt with a large "H" on the front instead of the normal super-hero "S." My son, Cody, suggested I wear the T-shirt whenever I preached the huper message. The rest is history . . . Huperman was born!

I believe everyone has a life message that is stamped in their DNA and stirred up in their calling. It's the theme woven through life's lessons and longings. No matter where you go or what you do, a watermark of significance emerges. Huperman is just this message for me.

This revised edition marks the fifteenth anniversary of the original *Huperman* book. By the grace of God, my story has traveled around the world from Africa to Vietnam and from Europe to South America. It has inspired average, ordinary people to live an extraordinary life by God's supernatural power. I am continually surprised when I meet people who have heard my story from restrooms to boardrooms. In the British Airways Executive Club lounge in Heathrow Airport, before boarding a flight to Asia, a man ran after me calling out, "Hey, you're Huperman!" He had seen a replay of the Huperman sermon broadcast on television in Brussels.

The testimonies have significantly exceeded my expectations and imagination! They are vast and vary from country to country. One man dreamed of being a fireman and overcame the fear of being too old and received multiple job offers. Athletes wore their HUPERMAN shirt under their uniforms to remind them of their huper strength to excel in their sport. It has inspired many parents of cleft lip and cleft palate children to believe God to see huper purpose through this challenge.

I am sorry to say, I don't remember the Great Grimsby lady's name, and most likely, she has since gone on to be with Jesus; but on behalf of all of us touched by the Huperman message, we say, "Thank you! What you thought was small and insignificant, God used in a big way!" Great things can shine out of grim vessels when His glory gets involved.

[PART 1]

HUPER PRINCIPLES

GOD WANTS TO TAKE YOU BEYOND normal, beyond reasonable, and beyond what's expected. This book is about how to do just that! In Part One, we'll discover keys from 2 Corinthians 4:7–18 to unlock God's *huper* power within us. Second Corinthians 4:7 KJV says, *"But we have this treasure in earthen vessels, that the excellency of the power may be of God, and not of us."* The Greek word for "excellency" here is our HUPER word, *huperbole*, which means an exaggeration or "throwing beyond." **That exaggeration or HUPER power is God's grace working in us to release His glory through us.** These verses provide a blueprint for the HUPER life Jesus died to give us. Walk with me as I share my story and reveal how these HUPER verses can transform your life beyond ordinary to God's extraordinary purpose through you.

Huperbole: (hü-per-bo-lā) *"a throwing beyond" (huper, "over," ballo, "to throw"), denotes "excellence, exceeding greatness," of the power of God in His servants* (Vine's Dictionary)[1]

But we have this treasure in earthen vessels, that the excellence of the power may be of God and not of us. We are hard-pressed on every side, yet not crushed; we are perplexed, but not in despair; persecuted, but not forsaken; struck down, but not destroyed—always carrying about in the body the dying of the Lord Jesus, that the life of Jesus also may be manifested in our body. For we who live are always delivered to death for Jesus' sake, that the life of Jesus also may be manifested in our mortal flesh. So then death is working in us, but life in you. And since we have the same spirit of faith, according to what is written, "I believed and therefore I spoke," we also believe and therefore speak, knowing that He who raised up the Lord Jesus will also raise us up with Jesus, and will present us with you. For all things are for your sakes, that grace, having spread through the many, may cause thanksgiving to abound to the glory of God. Therefore we do not lose heart. Even though our outward man is perishing, yet the inward man is being renewed day by day. For our light affliction, which is but for a moment, is working for us a far more exceeding and eternal weight of glory, while we do not look at the things which are seen, but at the things which are not seen. For the things which are seen are temporary, but the things which are not seen are eternal. (2 Cor. 4:7–16)

BREAKING BARRIERS

> *However ordinary each of us may seem, we are all in some way special, and can do things that are extraordinary, perhaps until then . . . impossible."*
> —Roger Bannister

IMPOSSIBLE. No man could run a mile under four minutes . . . until May 6, 1954. Experts said it was humanly impossible. The human body could not perform such a feat. They called it an unattainable limit—a barrier that could not be broken. But, on that ordinary spring day in 1954, an Oxford medical student from Harrow on the Hill named Roger Bannister broke through the barrier. The race announcer yelled, "The time was three . . . " The crowd erupted with jubilant cheers before finishing with "59.4 seconds." On that day, three minutes and 59.4 seconds entered the history books. [1]

The previous record had stood for over nine years, but Bannister's record lasted just forty-six days. What was once deemed inconceivable was now attainable. Australian John Landy was the second man to break the barrier by running the mile in 3:58. Once broken, the barrier became a drawbridge for others to cross. In 1964, American Jim Ryun became the first high school student to break the barrier. In 2017, Norwegian Jakob Ingebrigtsen became the youngest to join the sub-four-mile club at sixteen. Interestingly, he had two brothers who also ran under four minutes. What was previously deemed impossible was now in the realm of possibility. What was once the ceiling now became the floor.

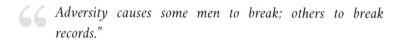

> *Adversity causes some men to break; others to break records."*

- WILLIAM ARTHUR WARD

If a man can break these barriers physically, how much more can we overcome with the supernatural strength of a living God? His strength has no limits or boundaries, from glory to glory. The universe is still expanding on his command. No matter what you've seen him do in the past, He has something bigger and better up his sleeves. And yes, He has big sleeves! The question is not if He can, but if we believe He can—through us!

SUPERSONIC

Until 1947, no one had ever flown faster than the speed of sound. Bullets and cannonballs could remain stable at supersonic speeds, but no one knew if a plane or a human, when pushed to those limits, could handle the pressure. Many pilots not only failed but died attempting to conquer the "demon." Air Force war hero and test pilot Chuck Yeager had tried six times and failed, each time inching closer to the elusive speed of Mach 1. Two days before his seventh attempt, on October 12, Yeager fractured his ribs while horseback riding. Determined to remain on the mission, he snuck away to a local veterinarian to have his ribs taped up so a doctor wouldn't know. Unable to close the hatch door because of excruciating pain, Chuck took a broom handle with a hook on the end to pull it down. Nothing would stop him. The X-1 plane, Glamorous Glennis, named after his wife, dropped from a huge B-29 aircraft and accelerated toward its goal of Mach 1.

Yeager's speed climbed to Mach 0.7 . . . then Mach 0.8 . . . and on toward Mach 0.9. The closer he got, the more violently the plane shook—and undoubtedly, the louder the voices in his head to turn back. Yeager later explained, "Just before you break through the sound barrier, the cockpit shakes the most." But he pushed through the opposition, pressing the plane's throttle with a determination to reach the impossible. Suddenly, it happened! A loud sonic *boom* thundered through the Mojave Desert. Chuck Yeager had reached Mach 1. He had broken the sound barrier! It was like a poke through Jell-O, or as Chuck described it, "as smooth as a baby's bottom." All the opposition was on the front end.

"Leveling off at 42,000 feet, I had thirty percent of my fuel, so I turned on rocket chamber three and immediately reached .96 Mach. I noticed that the faster I got, the smoother the ride. Suddenly the Mach needle began to fluctuate. It went up to .965 Mach—then tipped right off the scale . . . We were flying supersonic. And it was as smooth as a baby's bottom; Grandma could be sitting up there sipping lemonade." [2] - Chuck Yeager

There was no fanfare. It was a secret mission; few people watched. Yeager was strictly forbidden to tell anyone what took place that day. But that didn't change the fact—or the truth—that on October 14, 1947, what had been deemed impossible had become a reality. Yeager had literally gone where no one had dared go before. By the 1950s, many combat aircraft could routinely break the sound barrier in level flight, and later, commercial jets could. Now a land vehicle and even parachuting humans have slain the demon. We live in a time where space travel and supersonic speeds are the norms, but it all started with that first *boom*!

Exceeding Himself

You may have heard it said, "Yesterday's excellence is today's standard and tomorrow's mediocrity." Even our Father, the universe architect, exceeds Himself. How is that even possible?

Our God is an exceeding God. Throughout the Bible, we see God in action providing for the salvation of mankind. In the Old Testament, the death of the lamb always provided salvation, and with each lamb, each deliverance was exceedingly, abundantly above the former deliverance. Bishop Tony Miller says it this way: "One lamb was offered for one man—for Isaac on the mount. Then, one lamb was slain for a household—the children of Israel in Egypt. Then, a lamb was offered for a whole nation—Israel, each year on the Day of Atonement. Finally, one Lamb was crucified for all mankind—Jesus on the cross."

- One lamb = one man (Isaac)
- One lamb = a household (Egypt)
- One lamb = a whole nation (Israel on the Day of Atonement)
- One Lamb = all mankind—Jesus on the cross!

You may say, "Well, there you go. God can't exceed that!" However, think about this: More people are alive on the planet today than in the history of mankind. So, the blood of Jesus is doing more to redeem mankind today than ever before in history. And tomorrow, it will do even more, and the next day, it will do more; and so on and so on. God is an exceedingly, abundantly beyond

God. He always has something else up His sleeves. (If He had sleeves, they'd be big sleeves!) He is the Almighty One, the Ancient of Days who has been and will always be, from glory to glory! (Can I get an amen?) We serve a God who is in the barrier-breaking business! Although God created the universe with natural limitations, He is not restrained, restricted, or regulated by them. As an omnipresent, omnipotent, and omniscient God, His only barrier is His Word.

> *In Christ, we aren't breaking the sound barrier but the SEEN barrier! We break seen barriers by looking at unseen realities."*

Our limits, on the other hand, are innumerable—even with our untapped manifold human potential. But what is impossible with man is possible with God! (See Luke 18:27.) Abraham and Sarah had a baby. Moses parted a sea. Elijah outran a chariot. (Maybe he was actually the first four-minute miler!) David killed a giant with a slingshot. Esther saved a nation. Joshua won a battle with heaven's hailstones. Peter walked on water. Our Father delights in making us, His children, the exception to the natural rule. In Christ, we aren't breaking the sound barrier but the "seen" barrier! Just as Yeager broke what they referred to as the "sound demon," we break the power of every demon limiting us to what we *see* in the natural that's stopping us. We break *seen barriers* by looking at *unseen realities*!

Our enemy, who comes to steal, kill, and destroy tries to contain us with natural limits—what we can see, hear, feel, taste, and touch. These limits are like lids that shrink us down and contain us. They could be physical barriers like health, finances, or circumstances; but the strongest limits are the mental barriers that talk us out of our own miracle mile. These are mentalities that sound like, "It'll never work out for me . . . if only I had more . . . if only I were younger . . . if only I lived somewhere else . . . if only I finished school . . . if only I wasn't divorced. . . ." You fill in the blank to name your lid. As you can see, the focus here is on "I" and not the "I AM." I believe God's about to lift the lid with a revelation of his power in your weakness!

My LID = "If only I _____."

Many people like Robert Bannister and Chuck Yeager have amazed us with their impossible efforts. History is filled with barrier-breaking people who specialized in making possible what others said could not be done. If these great things are possible in human strength, what kind of crazy, impossible things can be done partnering with God's power? God is a barrier-breaking God!

Are you ready to launch past the seen barrier into your breakthrough? Are you ready to free the potential inside you and lift the lid to the excuses limiting you?

2

ONE BOY'S STORY: TRADING DEFECTS FOR DESTINY

> *Eye has not seen, nor ear heard, nor have entered into the heart of man the things which God has prepared for those who love Him."*
> —1 Cor. 2:9

EVERYONE HAS A STORY. I believe every God-created human has a divine purpose written by the hand of God before they were born. That purpose has a unique theme woven into His kingdom's story for a distinct time, people, and place. The devil attacks at that point of destiny and attempts to thwart God's original design and ultimately hinder the display of His glory on the earth. Look for the places of contention and challenges, and you'll find clues to the unmined gold inside.

Most mothers cry tears of joy when their children are born. On February 27, 1967, my mother cried, but they were tears of shock and dismay. This was her second birth. My sister was born almost five years earlier without defect, and no one suspected that my story would start any different. We had no known history of birth defects on either side of my family. Imagine her surprise when she was handed a baby boy with a severe cleft lip and palate. Today in modernized countries, this birth defect is routinely repaired through surgical procedures, but in the 1960s this wasn't the case.

I had a gaping hole in the roof of my mouth and a unilateral cleft lip, which means I had large holes in my upper lip that went up through my nose. In that era, children born with this abnormality had severe speech impediments, ear infections, feeding difficulties, dental problems, and needed multiple surgeries to repair the missing tissue. In addition to the physical anguish, maybe more difficult was the taboo sense of societal shame. They took no pictures of me to censor the unnatural deviation.

My mother's grief wasn't just because she'd never seen a child like this. Her greatest sorrow was the loss of the future she had imagined for me. Her father, Dr. Marvin Earnheart, was a respected pastor and radio preacher, and she prayed that I would continue the legacy of his ministry. *How could I preach if I couldn't speak?*

Hospitals became a necessary evil for me. It's hard for a child to understand why pain is the best option for their healing. By the time I was ten years old, I had multiple excruciating surgeries. I have a scar on my right side, where they took out a piece of a rib to create the hard palate for my mouth. I remember how after one surgery the doctor came in to remove the gauze packed into my nasal cavity. It seemed like he had already pulled out fifty feet of gauze, and I begged them to stop and put me to sleep so I couldn't feel what seemed like never-ending torture. They said it wasn't necessary and it wouldn't hurt much. Apparently, they had never had that done to themselves because I remember screaming in anguish. It literally felt like someone was pulling my brains through my nose!

One time, a nurse was simply removing an IV from my arm when blood began to squirt all over my face and the bed—probably as a result of something I did, but this became another traumatic experience that fed an irrational fear of needles and all things medical. (I'm still not the best person to call for hospital visits, but it is beautifully redemptive that my daughter is now a nurse.)

WHY AM I SO DIFFERENT?

I am extremely thankful for all the surgeons and medical professionals who repaired my face. Despite many surgeries, my nose is a bit flat and makes me look like I collided with a Mack truck. Growing up, this made me an easy target for kids to make fun of. As an adult, my wife and I moved back to my hometown of Decatur, Texas, with our kids for a season. Driving my kids to school, I passed by the same playgrounds where I was bullied and picked on as a child. As I looked at the same old tired playground equipment, I pictured that scared little boy battling the bullies. They said things like, "You're so ugly. You will never amount to anything, you hare-lipped boy!" I remember looking in the mirror and thinking, *Why am I different? Why am I like this? Why do I have to go to the hospital?*

Regular trips to the orthodontist were also necessary because teeth grew in the roof of my mouth. Some grew in backward and required chains and mechanisms to expand my jaw. These things hurt so bad I thought my head would explode. As a young boy, I remember crying over and over and saying, "I don't understand. Why do I have to go through this?"

My grandfather, the preacher, was my boyhood hero and mentor. He pastored churches for over fifty years and preached his last message at ninety-three after overcoming three heart attacks. The bright side of orthodontist trips was riding in the car, just him and me. He drove an hour from Dallas to pick me up and take me to the appointments. Back and forth, time after time, we traveled together. On the way, he told me stories about the goodness of God.

I remember riding in the car one day with him, and I said, "Paw-paw, why do I have to go through all this?"

He said, "Honey, I don't really understand that either, but I believe God has a great plan for your life and will give you the strength to overcome any obstacle."

As we talked ride after ride, something started stirring and rising up in my spirit. They were talks of truth that changed my life. One day I prayed, "God, I refuse to be defined by these limits anymore!" In my mind, I knew the limits were still there, but something was changing. I was starting to believe I was born for something greater than what I was experiencing at the moment. I prayed, "I don't look right and people make fun of me, but if You will just anoint me . . . if You will just empower me . . . if You just help me, then I will go anywhere You tell me to go. I will do anything You tell me to do. I'll say anything You tell me to say." The reality of God's truth rose up in my heart and strengthened me against the struggle.

STRENGTH FOR THE STRUGGLE

When I was twelve years old, my dad left my mom, and they went through a bitter divorce. I remember staring in disbelief at the woodpile where my dad took me to tell me he was leaving. How could my life go from bad to worse? I remember thinking, *Now, I don't even have a dad. How am I ever going to make it?*

My mom struggled to pay the bills and battled depression. Some days she couldn't get out of bed, so my sister cooked and cared for all of us. A dark cloud closed in on us, and one desperate day, I sat on the living room floor with a gun in my hand. Ominous thoughts jeered at me from the bully of all bullies: *Go ahead, take your life.*

Leave a note begging your parents to get back together. Go ahead, it's the only way. This would be the greatest thing you could do with your life. The enemy assaulted me with vain imaginations and lies to cut off my destiny and deeply wound those I loved. This lie taunted me and tried to exalt itself above the truth. Thankfully, after contemplating the option, I came to my senses and put the gun away and prayed for God to help me.

For every lie the devil sent directly or disguised in other people's hurtful words, God sent people with words of truth. A light shone through our dark days when we were invited to a small, but spirited, church. My grandfather was a Fundamental Baptist, and I was not acquainted with things of this "Holy Spirit" they spoke of. Pastor Robert Douglas saw something special in me and the potential of God's purpose. I prayed to be filled with the Holy Spirit, and a new dimension opened in me. Just like when Chuck Yeager pushed through the sound barrier, the anointing pushed me through all the torment and trouble into God's presence and promise.

Most adults my age who had a cleft lip and palate have a severe lisp, and it's hard to understand them. Miraculously, as a baby, I received experimental surgery at a children's hospital in Dallas. (Ironically, years later, my youngest daughter would be selected to do a nursing externship at that very hospital.) This surgery significantly helped me overcome the speech impediment. We traveled from my hometown to the big city of Denton for a speech test at Texas Woman's University. The therapist told my mom that I had no impediment and sent us on our way. I'm sure God was smiling that day in anticipation of what was to come. Years later, on that same TWU campus, that once scared little boy would stand in faith and launch the first services of The Bridge Church!

> *I may not be the most exegetical, hermeneutical, and homiletical preacher you'll ever hear, but I might be the most thankful."*

Today I joke that if you think I talk funny, it's not genetic from my defect—it's environmental because I'm from Texas! When I tell my story, I always say, *"I may not be the most exegetical, hermeneutical, and homiletical preacher you'll ever hear, but I might be the most thankful."*

BEYOND IMAGINATION

Many times, when I'm speaking about Ephesians 3:20 and God's huper plan for their life, I'll tell people to close their eyes and think for a minute of the wildest thing they can imagine God doing in their life. Then I'll say, "Open your eyes . . . it's beyond that. Huper is exceedingly, abundantly, and above what you could ask, think, or even imagine—a whole other level that's impossible to comprehend in a human heart."

As a boy I feared that I'd never find a wife who would love me and accept me. I feared I'd never be a father or that I could be a good father. I didn't know what I'd do to support myself. All I had was a tiny glimmer of God's call to live beyond myself—and the Holy Spirit to help me! I love how 1 Corinthians 2:9-10 sums it up.

"Eye has not seen, nor ear heard, nor have entered into the heart of man the things which God has prepared for those who love Him. But God has revealed them to us through His Spirit. For the Spirit searches all things, yes, the deep things of God."
(1 Cor. 2:9–10)

God reached down and found me, a troubled boy abandoned at the woodpile, and invited me into greater possibilities than human DNA provides. It's like turning a nervous and apprehensive Clark Kent into the invincible Superman . . . or HUPERMAN. God's huper anointing turned a frail and flawed jar into a vessel that could display His glory. Let's learn more about the treasure that transforms us from average to awesome.

3

TREASURE EXPOSED

> *But we have this treasure in earthen vessels, that the excellency of the power may be of God, and not of us."*
> —2 Cor. 4:7 KJV

VESSELS ARE DESIGNED to hold something; without it, they are empty and without purpose. Genesis tells us how God formed the first vessel out of a handful of dust. The Master Potter sculpted Adam, the first human prototype, because He longed for a son. Like Geppetto crafted the puppet Pinocchio, God squeezed out the shape of humanity, hollowing out his heart to hold a sample of the treasure, the presence of the divine. The Adam vessel rested empty and hollow until the Father *"breathed into his nostrils the breath of life..."* (Gen. 2:7 NIV), and then he became a living being—containing and carrying the breath of God! The purpose of the jar was fulfilled; hollowed out to hold heaven's hope.

"*But we have this treasure in earthen vessels, that the excellency of the power may be of God, and not of us*" (2 Cor. 4:7 KJV). Before the "but" at the start of this verse, Paul is encouraging the Corinthians to *"not lose heart"* (v. 1). Only one reason can embolden us. We're not alone. We're not limited to our dirt, our clay, and our humanness. There is a light that shines on our humanity. We hold hope!

> *But God chose us, earthen vessels, because the whole point was not to hide the treasure but to expose it."*

If it were up to me, I don't think I'd put the treasure of God in a clay, human jar. I'd pick something more secure to house priceless treasure. Something like Fort Knox or the Tower of London would be more fitting. But God chose us, earthen vessels, because the whole point was not to hide the treasure but to expose it! He uses clay jars to exhibit "the excellency" of His power (v. 7). The Greek word for excellency here is our HUPER word, huperbole, (pronounced hü-per-bo-lā). As I explained in my Introduction and Part One, it means a *"throwing beyond, exceeding greatness, or an exaggeration."* It's like our word hyperbole. A hyperbole is an extravagant exaggeration.

> **Huperbole:** (hü-per-bo-lā) *"a throwing beyond"* (huper, *"over,"* ballo, *"to throw"*), denotes *"excellence, exceeding greatness,"* of the power of God in His servants. - Vine's Dictionary

When my kids were teenagers, they were great at using hyperbole. Everything was extreme. Everything was the "-est." If a room was a little warm, "it was the *hottest* room in the world!" If a room was a little chilly, "it was the coldest place on earth!" If they wanted a snack, they were starving! They took it to the extra extreme—no middle road. God wants to make our lives one huge hyperbole, beyond ourselves for His glory! He wants the *exaggeration* to be "of God" and not "of us," so when He does something outrageous in our life, people say, "That *must* be God, that cannot be them!"

God uses ordinary, average people to do extraordinary things. Why? So He gets the glory! But how does the treasure come out? Just like in Gideon's story, it has to be broken. Broken does not mean ruined; it can be the experience that lets the light shine through.

SMASHING JARS

Judges 7 tells the story of Gideon, the self-proclaimed weakest vessel of them all who questioned God's choice of using him to overcome the enemies harassing Israel. Gideon saw his weakness, his fear, and his doubts about himself. God saw a vessel he could get His glory through. Israel loved heroes who rallied their egos to fight —God wanted a see-through vessel who could display His glory. I don't think much has changed today.

Often the church is tempted to follow leaders who appear to have it all together. We fall into the trap that their highlight reel is all their life is made of; their Instagram stories are the entire stories of their lives. This can make us feel "less than." We are comparing their highlight reel to our entire game. The truth is, in our own strength, we are all Gideons; we are all pretty ordinary without God! And maybe, just maybe, God's more interested in using damaged, "coming apart" cardboard boxes than "put together" porcelain jars.

God plans to use Gideon to save Israel, but first He lays off most of the army. He starts with thirty-two thousand men, and before the day is over He charges Gideon to lead three hundred men to attack the Midianites. Why in the world would God fire 98 percent of the troops? He tells Gideon, *"You have too many men. I cannot deliver Midian into their hands, or Israel would boast against me, 'My own strength has saved me'"* (Judg. 7:2 NIV).

God chose to use a weak vessel to show off His strength to the people. (Is there something you have too much of that prevents God from showing off in your life? Just wondering.) After receiving courage from the Lord, Gideon gave each of his three hundred men a trumpet and an empty jar with torches inside. At his signal, Gideon told the men to sound the trumpet and smash the jars so the torches would shine. In unison they shouted, *"The sword of the Lord and of Gideon!"* as they miraculously defeated the enemy (Judg. 7:20). That day, Israel experienced God's victory by yielding their vulnerability.

To get a treasure out of a jar, first the treasure has to be exposed. One way to expose the treasure is to smash the jar. I don't believe it's the heart of our Father God to go around smashing jars, but Jesus told us that *"in this life we will have trouble"* (John 16:33, author's paraphrase), and He is ready to rescue us and turn that trouble into triumph.

Caveman Theology

I love sharing my "caveman theology" as I speak around the world; it is one of my favorite things to do. Seeing it translated into different languages can be hilarious. It's simple. It's so easy that even a caveman can learn it. Are you ready? "God good! Devil bad!" I told you it was simple. After saying it in a slow, exaggerated Neanderthal voice, I make everyone else shout it and grunt like a caveman. UUUuuuugg! Now you try it—it's very therapeutic. God Goooooooood! Devil BAAAAA-AAD! UUUuuuugg! (Note: You have to make fists with both hands and then pull them back quickly when you do the caveman grunt!)

Got it? It's meant to be comic relief, but we complicate the gospel too much. So many times in life, there are things we don't understand, but this helps us remember the simple yet transforma-tive power of the gospel. If we can keep it this simple, it invigorates our joy in life. God is always good, and the devil is always bad. God's goodness redeems all the bad things in me. *"The Lord is good to all, and His tender mercies are over all His works"* (Ps. 145:9).

Now, I come from a particular theological stance that says God doesn't go around breaking jars. Some people disagree with that stance, and that's fine—we all have our opinions. I don't believe God gives people things like cancer to prove a point. I don't believe God abuses His children to teach them lessons. I believe if a jar gets broken, the devil is the one who breaks it. He tries to push you into a corner and beat you down. His goal is to define you, to limit you, and finally, to defeat you. So he piles up the trouble in your life to try to overwhelm and destroy you. When the devil intends some-thing for evil, God turns the tables and uses it for your good—so much so, that it can look like it was God's plan all along. God doesn't have to be the author of something to be the Lord of it!

> *God doesn't have to be the author of something to be the Lord of it!"*

Your abuse, tragedy, bankruptcy, or divorce may not have been from the hand of God, but if He becomes the Lord of it, then His grace and goodness are authorized to flow from it!

HARD-PRESSED ON EVERY SIDE

As Christians, we hear a lot about this treasure Paul speaks of. We know the resurrection life of Jesus is in us through salvation. We love 2 Corinthians 4:7, but what about the verses that follow? We've got to keep reading to experience transformation. The apostle Paul was authorized with great authority to speak beyond verse 7. He experienced firsthand how the "surpassing power" is revealed or squeezed out by the pressure around us. To get to life, we go through death.

"We are hard-pressed on every side, yet not crushed; we are perplexed, but not in despair; persecuted, but not forsaken; struck down, but not destroyed always carrying about in the body the dying of the Lord Jesus, that the life of Jesus also may be manifested in our body."
(2 Cor. 4:8–10)

Let's break this down:

- **Pressed** = This literally means "hemmed in" but not restricted; crowded, but not crushed. The *King James Version* says, "troubled but not distressed." Life's stress and people's opinions provide a full-court press on our emotions, but God provides the energy to keep moving toward the goal and to not crumble under pressure!
- **Perplexed** = The Greek word means "to stand in doubt." It means you can't decide which way to go or what to do. It especially implies to be at a loss mentally and feel utterly embarrassed and without hope. We may face "perplexing" situations, but we always have hope!
- **Persecuted** = Persecuted here means to be pursued, chased after and run down, and mistreated. Forsaken is to be left behind, forgotten, and abandoned. You may be chased by the enemy, but we will never be forsaken by the Father.
- **Pushed Down** = Some translations say struck down, cast down, or knocked down. It implies a hurling to the

ground or to a lower stance. Think Rocky Balboa here!
You may get knocked down, but you are not knocked out!
You may lose a battle, but in Christ, you have won the
war.

Can you relate to any of these? I used to read this verse and
think "Oh, man, this is so terrible!" Today I see Paul's words in a
different light. He says in verse 10 that we are always bearing about
in our body the dying of the Lord Jesus, that the life of Jesus might
be made manifest in our body.

> *"We continually share in the death of Jesus in our own bodies so
> that the resurrection life of Jesus will be revealed through our
> humanity."*
> (2 Cor. 4:10 TPT)

I like how Leonard Sweet says, *"Crisis and trials in life can either
break you down or break you open"* (11 Indispensable Relationships You
Can't Be Without).[1] This confuses many Christians who expect life
on earth to be like a ride at Disney World instead of a life-and-death
battle. There's no "easy button." You're going to want to quit and
stop believing there's any way *you* can overcome or make a difference. There at the bottom of that desperation, you realize *you* can't,
but there's someone *in you* that can! Our adversity can actually
reveal the resurrection life of God in us. When I get to the end of
me, I find the beginning of God.

> *Is your trouble working for you, or are you working for
> your trouble? Your trouble can actually reveal the treasure!"*

Now, here is a man—the apostle Paul—who was shipwrecked,
stoned, knocked in the head, bitten by a snake, and left for dead. In
verse 17 of 2 Corinthians 4, he called these trials *"light and momen-*

tary affliction," and I get upset when my satellite TV doesn't work! He says our temporary affliction is working for us a far more exceeding and eternal weight of glory. Is your trouble working for you, or are you working for your trouble? Your trouble can actually reveal the treasure!

GET YOUR TROUBLE WORKING FOR YOU

David made a ridiculous faith declaration as he faced his taunting foe, Goliath. In 1 Samuel 17:46, David says, *"This day the LORD will deliver you into my hands, and I'll strike you down and cut off your head..."* (NIV). That is a bold statement for a little boy who doesn't even own a pocketknife! With rocks in his hand and faith in his heart, David believed the trouble coming *at* him was not stronger than the power *with* him. The weapon in Goliath's hand designated to kill David became the sword that David used to kill Goliath. God used the very sword designed to destroy David to deliver him!

> *God used the very sword designed to destroy David to deliver him!"*

As for me, the devil thought, "I will give this boy a cleft lip and palate. I will slap him around a little bit. I will abuse him. I will have kids make fun of him. I'll have his parents break up." The enemy thought he was digging a grave to bury me in my circumstances. But as the dirt piled up inch by inch, God was turning the tables. The soil dug out of the ground to bury me created a platform to praise Him and promote His glory. My grave became my dance floor. What tried to bury me built a platform to proclaim His goodness.

What has tried to bury you? What has the Enemy used to destroy your destiny and overwhelm your opportunity? Most people think their trouble disqualifies them from victory, or they use it as an excuse not to press through the barriers. God wants to use your trouble to transform you! What you thought disqualified you can actually catapult you through the limits into the exaggeration of God's grace! What if your disqualification is actually your invitation to display His glory through you? Just like Gideon, what you think is your disadvantage might be your place of greater trust, which reveals the greater treasure!

The soil dug out of the ground to bury me created a platform to proclaim His glory.

We can either be consumed by our pain, or we can use our pain to produce the glory of God—His anointing in our life. Two people can go through the same or similar trial. One will come out with a testimony, and the other will gain trouble and tragedy. What makes the difference is how they let it work *for* them (in God's hand to reveal His glory) or *against* them (by the devil's plan to destroy them).

As you read the next chapter, I pray for you to have a "great reckoning" to see where your breakdown is actually God's plan to break you open and display His glory in the earth. Just as Paul said, *"What worked death in you, brings life to others"* (2 Cor. 4:12, author's paraphrase). Life - Death - Life. We have the treasure (life of God) *in* us, and then the enemy tries to kill us (death), but what was meant to kill us, *releases* the treasure *in* us and causes the life of God to flow *through* us! So the circle of resurrection life ensues.

> *All God's giants have been weak men who did great things for God because they reckoned on God being with them."*
>
> — HUDSON TAYLOR

We are like common clay jars that carry this glorious treasure within, so that the extraordinary overflow of power will be seen as God's, not ours. Though we experience every kind of pressure, we're not crushed. At times we don't know what to do, but quitting is not an option. We are persecuted by others, but God has not forsaken us. We may be knocked down, but not out. We continually share in the death of Jesus in our own bodies so that the resurrection life of Jesus will be revealed through our humanity. (2 Cor. 4:7–10 TPT)

4

OUT OF THE BOX & INTO CHRIST

> " *For we who live are always delivered to death for Jesus'*
> *sake, that the life of Jesus also may be manifested in our*
> *mortal flesh."*
>   —2 Cor. 4:11

I CLOSED my eyes and tried to fall asleep on the living room sofa, or settee as they call it in Bujumbura, Burundi. I was visiting my good friends, missionaries to Africa, Jamie and Lea Peters, to train children's workers. Just days before I met my brother and sister-in-law, Ross and Amy Weatherford, and Ralph Hagemeier, my long-time missionary friend and mentor in Kalemie, DRC, where Ralph established a Bible school and church. After ministering for a few days there, we all journeyed back across the vast Lake Tanganyika to Kigoma, Tanzania, and took a tiny Mission Aviation Fellowship (MAF) plane to Bujumbura. The night was dark, but there was lots of activity outside. I turned over on the sofa, and tried to ignore the reality happening beyond the gate outside.

Civil war between the Hutu and Tutsi tribes raged uncontrollably. The streets were barricaded, bombs would unexpectedly go off, and ambushes were set—the gunfire, or "music," was usually in the distance. All foreigners were instructed to vacate for their safety. There was one problem. Jamie and Lea followed the Word of the Lord, not the word of the American Embassy. If they weren't leaving, then how could I?

Jamie and Lea's church, Trinity Church International, was experiencing an amazing revival in the midst of uncertain political upheaval and genocide. The Peters truly were pressed, perplexed, and persecuted, but the presence of God sustained them with miraculous encounters of protection and healing. How could they leave now when God was doing so much?

I heard movement outside. I lay frozen still. Darkness assisted the rebels, or youth gangs, in raiding unsuspecting civilians. I was no stranger to uncomfortable and faith-stretching mission adventures. I ministered in Honduras during the Iran Contra conflict when tensions were high and, reportedly, there was a price on American heads. I spent a month traveling up and down the Amazon and Marañón River in Peru while the Shining Path terrorist group was known for their violence and guerrilla warfare. We preached in a hut overflowing with people, lit by one sixty-watt light bulb. It drew the attention of lots of mosquitos and the local witch doctor, who threatened us but then received Jesus when his wife was miraculously healed. I was never fearful obeying where God sent me before, but this night in Burundi was different.

Gunfire. It was coming from the house next door. The youth gang started banging our gate and threatening our house security guard. I could hear them shooting up the house next door. I also heard our petrified guard throwing up outside out of fear as they commanded he open the gate and come outside. My mind raced, not so much out of fear but out of serious reckoning of my life. The only things separating me from the attackers were a plate glass window and a concrete wall.

Before, when I was young and single, the thought of martyrdom was heroic; but now I was a husband and a dad. I thought of my kids back in Texas. At that time, we only had two. How would they remember me? Kelsey, with her blonde curls and blue eyes, was only three years old and a daddy's girl, and my son, Cody, was a one-year-old and wouldn't know or remember me. I prayed to God that if something happened to me, my kids would know their daddy didn't die from a heart attack climbing the corporate ladder, or die trying to get a bass boat or a bigger house to keep up with the neighbors. Their dad gave his life to preach the gospel to a hurting world.

That eventful night in 1995 was a defining moment: Something died in me. I died to my own ambition, to my way and will and desire to spotlight my plans. We've talked about how "we died when Christ died" when we're born again, but in every disciple's life, at some point we must choose to identify with the death and "reckon" it dead in us. The pressing exposed the true light of Jesus within me, not the spotlight of my own manufacturing. I determined that night to never get comfortable and to rely on His supernatural strength for an extraordinary life. If I didn't have something to die for, did I really have something to live for? We don't choose how or when we die, but we can choose how we live until we die. In my great reckoning, my jar was breaking open . . .

Get out of the Box

I am no longer in Adam, but I am in Christ. I often use a funny illustration to clarify this point. Suppose I took a toy action figure and put it in a large cereal box? I close the lid and begin to do crazy things to the box. I shake it. I drop it. I jump on it. I throw it in the air. Tell me, what happens to the toy? I throw it several feet in the air, then it falls to the ground. My feet crush it, leaving it tattered. Why? Because the toy is in the box. And, whatever happens to the box, happens to the toy! Its location determines its condition!

Spiritually, a law explains this. It's called the law of heredity, and its principle is seen in Hebrews 7. The author tells us that Levi paid tithes to Melchizedek. In other words, Levi got credit for paying tithes to Melchizedek when Abram paid tithes to Melchizedek. How is that possible when Levi was Abraham's great grandson? He was not even alive when this event took place. Because, Hebrews says, he was in Abraham's loins.

> *Even Levi, who receives tithes, paid tithes through Abraham, so to speak, for he was still in the loins of his father when Melchizedek met him.* (Heb. 7:9, 10)

Before I was born, I was in my mother's womb. Before I was in my mother's womb, I was in my daddy's loins (to use good old *King James* verbiage). And before I was in my daddy's loins, I was in my granddaddy's loins, and so on—all the way back to Adam. I was born "in Adam."

So, everything that happened to Adam (mankind), happened to me. Just like whatever happened to the box (in our previous illustration) happened to our tiny action figure.

> *What shall we say then? Shall we continue in sin that grace may abound? Certainly not! How shall we who died to sin live any longer in it? Or do you not know that as many of us as were baptized into Christ Jesus were baptized into His death? Therefore we were buried with Him through baptism into death, that just as Christ was raised from the dead by the glory of the Father, even so we also should walk in newness of life.* (Rom. 6:1–4)

Some people think, *I'm a pretty good person. I've never killed anyone. I've never robbed a bank. I've never done this or that.* That may be a fact, but according to the law of heredity, that is not true. Since you are born "in Adam," then, just like Levi, your ancestors' decisions are credited to your spiritual account. Everything they did, you did, all the way down through your natural bloodline. And, unfortunately for you, the moment you committed one sin, you "agreed" with all the sins of all the previous generations all the way back to Adam.

> *So, once you are IN CHRIST, everything that happened to Christ happened to me."*

But the good news is that 2 Corinthians 5:17 says if any man be "in Christ," he is a new creature. So, once you are IN CHRIST, everything that happened to Christ happened to me. When He died, I died, spiritually. When He rose, I rose to new life! If He is seated in heavenly places, you are seated in heavenly places IN CHRIST! That is news worth shouting about! It's finished, but it must be transferred to your account. How can such a transaction be applied to my life?

THE GREAT RECKONING

Over and over in the New Testament, we see the phrases "in Him," "in Christ," "in the Lord," "in the Spirit," and "in whom." Well, that's you and me. If you are in Christ, you can put your name in those verses. Throughout his letter to the Romans, Paul talked about reckoning. The word "reckon" in Greek is an accounting term. It means "to balance the books," like a system of credits and debits.

> Reckon (Greek = *logizomai*) *count, compute, count over, to take*
> *into account, to pass to one's account, to impute, consider* [1]

We must reconcile some things in our thinking. What happens if you don't reconcile your bank statement properly? Your checks will bounce, or maybe you will have money you didn't know you had. The same happens when we don't reconcile our life as Christ's! Resources are available that aren't accessed! Notice how Romans 6:11 tells us to reckon ourselves dead to sin but alive to God.

> *For he who has died has been freed from sin. Now if we died with*
> *Christ, we believe that we shall also live with Him, knowing that*
> *Christ, having been raised from the dead, dies no more. Death no*
> *longer has dominion over Him. For the death that He died, He died*
> *to sin once for all; but the life that He lives, He lives to God.*
> *Likewise you also, <u>reckon</u> yourselves to be dead indeed to sin, but*
> *alive to God in Christ Jesus our Lord.* (Rom. 6:7–11, emphasis
> added)

I used to train horses with my uncle John. He would ask me, "You think you can ride that horse?" My answer better be, "Yes, I reckon I can!" (We still say "reckon" in Texas.) Can you stand in the face of fear that's intimidating you? I reckon. Can you overcome the lies of insecurity that have plagued your identity? I reckon. Can you overcome this battle? I reckon I can. Can you forgive those who have hurt you? In Christ, I reckon all things are possible to those who believe! If we reckon God's grace properly in life, we can access all that God has deposited into our spiritual account "in Christ." Look what Paul says here in Romans: *"Likewise you also, reckon your-selves to be dead indeed to sin, but alive to God in Christ Jesus our Lord"* (Rom. 6:11).

Grace is RECEIVED with a humble heart (James 4:6–7) and RECKONED in a renewed mind (Rom. 6:11).

And if I . . .

> RECEIVE it in my heart,
> RECKON it in my mind,
> RELEASE it out of my mouth,
> I will REALIZE it in my life!

Sometimes, you've got to learn to SAY SO! Years ago, our daughter Ashton Joy stayed with our friends Chris and Karla Dunn while we led a mission team to Romania. At breakfast, Chris started tickling his kids and asked three-year-old Ashton if she wanted him to tickle her. She has always been a bit precocious and answered, "No, if I want you to tickle me then I will say so." Okay. Chris shrugged and went on with the day. A few days later, Ashton started calling out, louder and louder, "SO . . . SO . . . I said, SO!" They couldn't figure out what she was talking about. Finally, she explained, "You said if I wanted you to tickle me to say SO. I'm saying SO!" Everyone laughed and got tickled. Ashton finally got tired of being left out of the fun and said so.

NEAR-DEATH EXPERIENCES

God's good grace has been provided on the cross, but it is our reckoning that confirms our relationship with Him. Believe in your heart and confess with your mouth (Rom. 10:9). *Say so!* In Christ, your account has been reconciled to heaven's.

Your DNA has been redeemed by the blood of Jesus. You are a new creation. The old has gone, and there is an abundance of life credited to your account! It's time to access it.

I believe Paul lived as a dead man—dead to his old life and alive in Christ. Paul told the church at Colossae, *"For you died, and your life is hidden with Christ in God"* (Col. 3:3). Your life is hidden. You're hidden, and YOU cannot be found. Most Christians have near-death experiences.

They almost die and then say, *"Oh, excuse me, what about this or that point?"* Your dead man doesn't have A POINT or OPINION. *"But, but—excuse me!"* No, your dead man doesn't have a BUT!

The challenge here is building our theology on the idea that we have two natures. We say, "I am fighting my old man. My 'old man' tried to rise up." *But, how can a dead man rise up?* If he is dead, he is dead. Paul said my old man was crucified with Christ (Rom. 6:6). Then Paul asked himself these questions: *"Why do I do the things that I don't want to do, and I don't do the things I want to do? And the things I want to do, I don't do; and the things I don't want to do, I do?"* (See Rom. 7:15–20).

You might think Paul was confused about it all. Sometimes, we all feel just like Paul. The truth is, we are not fighting the old man. We are fighting the memory of who we once were, and memories are powerful! My grandfather, who helped build my faith, passed away a few years ago, but his memory is still very much alive in me. When I hear the old hymn "Just as I Am," immediately I think of him. It was one of his favorite songs. When I think of my grandfather, he becomes so real; I can even smell him. He is right there with me. Why? Because memories are powerful. They can make us feel something right now that was in the past.

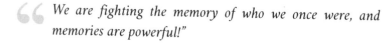

> *We are fighting the memory of who we once were, and memories are powerful!"*

Romans 12:2 instructs us to be transformed by renewing our minds so we won't be conformed to our old system of thinking, our old memory thought patterns. This is why Jesus said of communion, *"Do this in remembrance of me"* (Luke 22:19 NIV). The word "remember" is "to relive the experience all over again." When we remember the cross, we are reckoning it so in our lives. What's left of our old man is simply our memories. And, the more I can reckon what happened supernaturally when I became a new man in Christ, the more it manifests naturally.

The better we understand that we were broken 2,000 years ago in Christ, the more we can identify with His death and His resurrection. The SAME SPIRIT that raised Christ from the dead will quicken our mortal body (Rom. 8:11). Paul's perspective: "Go ahead and hit me with your best shot, devil, because all it will do is produce the resurrection life of Jesus in me. Devil, you cannot break my jar because my jar was broken when Christ's passion broke Him." If you have seen the movie *The Passion of the Christ*, you witnessed a graphic depiction of everything Jesus endured as He died. And because we are in Him, it happened to us. We died with Him. However, if I died with Him, then I must also be raised with Him! Why? Because if I am in Christ, then everything that happened to Him happened to me.

DELAYED BUT NOT DENIED

I began this chapter with the story of what God did in my heart one night amidst the "music" in Burundi, but I will end it with what He did in my heart through the "mundane" in Azle, Texas—when I had to stay home. Ten years before I ever went to Africa, our local church sponsored a team trip to the Congo. Africa was my destiny. I could taste it. I could feel it in my bones! It was calling me! I was anointed! I was ready! I asked my pastor and mentor, Kerry Wood, if I could be a part of the team. His response shocked me. He said, "No."

This test would either be my breaking down or my breaking open. I decided if I couldn't go, I was going to help someone else get there by giving. I would die to my dream to make someone else's come true. At the point of that setback, I couldn't see the harvest my seed would grow. My waiting in faith produced a "weight of glory" that was a true work of the Holy Spirit. Your "waiting" in faith produces a "weight of glory" that transforms your life beyond yourself.

Now I've ministered all over the continent of Africa so many times I can't remember the exact number. I've led multiple teams, started micro-finance projects, and partnered with hundreds of amazing churches, ministries, and leaders to preach the gospel, care for orphans, equip pastors, and feed the hungry. On top of that . . . are you ready for HUPER? I took my dad to Africa with me!

Talk about how all things are possible—with HIM! Only God could work a miracle like that! But, on that day of disappointment in 1985, God wasn't concerned about *MY* dream unfolding on the OUTSIDE, He was concerned about *HIS* dream unfolding on the INSIDE. His main priority was the work within the jar. Huper comes out of something that looks anything but HUPER! Miracles start in the mundane.

God is preparing you for what He has prepared for you—not in the spotlight, but in the dark room. He's developing you where it seems your dreams are dead. They're not dead, they are just planted. Sown in faith. When no one's looking, applauding, or cheering you on, miracles emerge in the mundane. Don't despise small beginnings or even seeming setbacks—make them work for you! You will see your "waiting" in faith produce a "weight of glory" that transforms your life beyond what you could ask, think, or imagine.

[5]

FACE THE FACTS, BUT EMBRACE THE TRUTH

> *While we do not look at the things which are seen, but at the things which are not seen. For the things which are seen are temporary, but the things which are not seen are eternal."*
> —2 Cor. 4:18

A TREMENDOUS NUMBER of facts tried to limit my life. Born with a birth defect, undergoing multiple surgeries, abandoned by my father, not enough money to pay our bills, ridiculed at school . . . the list of facts runs on and on; and these are just the FACTS. We're not even considering the lies the devil whispered. As I started yielding my life to the Holy Spirit, He began speaking TRUTH to my heart that was greater than the FACTS.

I have walked a lifelong journey trying to understand the difference between the truth and the facts and have learned a great deal along the way. The devil uses facts because they are in the natural in the SEEN realm. In our advanced digital age, information flies toward us at a staggering pace from news and entertainment networks, email, and social media. A 2018 study in *Forbes* magazine reported that 2.5 quintillion bytes of data are created each day and the pace accelerates daily.[1] When I was a kid, we watched the evening news and maybe read the morning paper for our daily facts of the world. You had to go find it. Now it comes to you all day long on your digital device of choice, notifying you of all the stressful situations you should worry about.

Psychologists are studying how "information overload" causes stress that can be detrimental to mental and physical health. Facts. Facts. Facts. Everywhere you turn, from CNN to the neighbor down the street, people are giving their opinion of the facts. So now we not only have the facts of the difficult situation but also everyone's opinion or spin according to their particular agenda.

As people of faith, we don't deny the facts. We can't bury our heads in the sand and say that something is not real, because we know the facts are evident. Sadly, this is where some well-meaning Christian teachers veered off by preaching that ignoring the FACTS was the only way to act in faith.

"For if you embrace the truth, it will release more freedom into your lives." (John 8:32 TPT)

The Cat Ate Your Bacon

My spiritual father, Pastor B. B. Hankins, used to tell a story about a pastor who made house visits to pray with people. His wife asked him to stop and get bacon for supper, so he spent his last few dollars to buy it and left it in the car while he made his last visit. Meanwhile, a stray cat crawled through the window into the backseat of the car and found the bacon. Upon returning to the car, the pastor caught the cat licking up the last piece of bacon. He got in the car and slammed the door, not wanting to return home without the bacon. He thought, *I'll try out this new faith thing.*

The pastor started declaring to the backseat with Sunday morning Pentecostal preacher passion, "That cat didn't eat my bacon! That cat didn't eat my bacon! That cat *did not* eat my bacon!" He turned around to look; the bacon was still gone. He tried again with even more zeal, but the smell of bacon was still fresh on the cat's lips. After a few more attempts, the pastor finally heard the Lord whisper, "The cat ate your bacon!" However, what the Lord said next changed everything: *"But don't worry. I have more bacon!"*

We aren't living in denial that facts and circumstances exist. We just refuse to embrace the facts as the final word. We understand there's a higher reality of God's eternal truth that's greater than the reality of our temporary situation.

Truth exists even when it is not manifested. By that I mean that certain things are true in the spirit realm, whether we ever see them manifested in the "seen" earth realm. It's like in 2 Kings 6 when Elisha prayed for his servant's eyes to be opened. *"Those who are with us are more than those who are with them"* (2 Kings 6:16 NIV). The servant saw the FACTS: The king's men surrounded the city with a full force of horses and chariots. Elisha saw the TRUTH—past the SEEN BARRIER. After he prayed, the servant saw the hills filled with horses and chariots of fire! There was a reality greater than the seen facts.

The Truth Can Change the Facts

Through the years, I have learned that facts never change the truth; however, God's truth, when applied properly, can change the facts.

We see this in 2 Corinthians 10:4–5, where Paul says, *"For the weapons of our warfare are not carnal, but mighty through God to the pulling down of strong holds; casting down imaginations, and every high thing that exalteth itself against the knowledge of God, and bringing into captivity every thought to the obedience of Christ"* (KJV).

Here, Paul gives us what I believe is a "backward" progression. He talks about:

1. Strongholds
2. Vain Imaginations
3. High Things
4. Thoughts

The enemy always begins with the fourth element: thoughts. He begins by putting a single thought into our minds. That, in itself, is relatively harmless, but it never remains a single thought. The thought, if not "captured" immediately, gathers friends (other thoughts) that soon begin to work in our minds. What are they doing? They are building "high things." The Greek word here is *hupsoma*, which literally means a "barrier" or "rampart."

High Thing (Greek = "*hupsoma*") *meaning elevated structure,*
barrier or bulwark [2]

The idea here: These thoughts are building a wall or barrier of
thought in the mind. The longer they hang around, the higher the
wall gets until finally it has "exalted itself" above the knowledge of
what God says about the situation (or we could say, "the truth").
Once they are high enough, the enemy begins to connect the walls
together and we form vain images in our minds. Paul calls these
"imaginations." The Greek word here is *logismos*, which means "a
reasoning that demands a verdict." The images that form from
thoughts now begin to demand a conclusion.

Vain Imaginations (Greek = *logismos*) *reasonings that bring a*
verdict hostile to Christian faith [3]

The problem: While this conclusion is congruent with the facts,
if its origins are from the enemy it is always contrary to the truth.
The result is that we end up with a "stronghold" in our minds. The
word "stronghold" in the original text is *ochuroma*, which literally
means "a fortress."

Stronghold (Greek = *ochuroma*) *a castle, fortress* [4]
The Aramaic word for strongholds can also be translated as
"rebellious castles." [5]

At this point, we are imprisoned in the castle of our own minds!
The enemy bombards us with mounds of facts piling up in front of
us until it's the only image we can see. Then we draw erroneous
conclusions from these facts. What is the answer?

Paul says the wall of thoughts is exalted above the "knowledge of
God." The only way out of our prison of thinking is to learn to exalt
the Truth above the Facts!

THE FACT MAY BE: You are sick in your body, but . . .
THE TRUTH IS: By Jesus's stripes, you are healed (Isa. 53:5)!
THE FACT MAY BE: Your finances are in horrible shape, but . . .
THE TRUTH IS: "My God shall supply all your needs according to His riches in glory" (Phil. 4:19).
THE FACT MAY BE: Your marriage is struggling and your child is away from God, but . . .
THE TRUTH IS: "As for me and my house, we will serve the Lord" (Josh. 24:15).

BE NOT AS THOUGH THEY WERE

You may say, "Duane, that is simply denial." No, it's not. And I'm not saying you should deny the facts. We face them. I'm saying you don't have to embrace them. In Romans 4, Paul says that Abraham, who the Bible calls the "Father of Faith," faced the fact that his body was as good as dead, but he believed God was able to perform what He had promised. When the facts said that Abraham couldn't perform, he believed God could! He exalted the truth of God's promise above the facts of his present condition.

Paul goes on to say this in Romans 4:17, "*As it is written, I have made thee a father of many nations, before him whom he believed, even God, who quickeneth the dead, and calleth those things which BE NOT AS THOUGH THEY WERE*" (KJV, emphasis added).

Paul understood that God calls those things that ARE NOT as though they are! Let me repeat that. God calls things that are not (yet manifested in the natural) as though they were (already manifested), not things that ARE (facts in the natural) as though they ARE NOT (which is denial)!

"God, who gives life to the dead and calls those things which do not exist as though they did...." (Rom. 4:17)

Like we learned in our "cat and bacon story," there was no power in denying the fact that the cat ate the pastor's bacon. The power was in declaring the greater truth! For example, if I say, "I'm not sick, I'm not sick, I'm not sick," over and over, that doesn't change the fact that I am sick. However, the power to change the facts lies in my believing and declaring over and over, "By Jesus's stripes I am healed."

GOD'S WORD IN MY MOUTH MOVES MOUNTAINS

Why? I am not denying the facts; I am exalting the truth! That's what happens when God prophetically declares great things over someone, even though that person may not be living it out. He is not denying their flaws; He is speaking things that are NOT (yet in the natural realm) as though they were already manifested. As the *New King James* says, *"and call those things which do not exist as though they did."* When God "calls" it, or speaks it, His voice has creative power. Only God can create something out of nothing, and how did He create it? He spoke it!

And since we have the same spirit of faith, according to what is written, "I believed and therefore I spoke," we also believe and therefore speak.... (2 Cor. 4:13)

This goes back to what we discovered in Chapter 3. We believe by our RECKONING and then we SPEAK. We say SO! We speak what we see in the supernatural, and our words are established in the natural. With this "same spirit of faith, we believe, therefore, we speak." This declaration of TRUTH exalts God's Word over the FACTS.

Relativity of Reckoning

Just as God created the universe when He spoke, your SAYING is your SOWING; it's your creative words in agreement with God's truth. Pastor, Bible teacher, and scientist Perrianne Brownback has been my go-to science fact finder for years. She expounds on cool things she's researched for days, and then I steal it and preach it all over the world! (Sounds like a great deal to me!) All joking aside, when she explained the similarity of the theory of relativity and faith to me, I was so astounded that I had to share it! I'm sure you're familiar with Einstein's theory of relativity . . .

$$E=mc^2$$

What if we looked at it this way? ENERGY equals the supernatural power of God to change something. MASS is the object of your faith or whatever you are believing for. The CONSTANT for Einstein was the speed of light, but for us it's the Word of God. Then SQUARED is God's Word in YOUR mouth. You "square" it when you speak it! God's Word in your mouth thrusts your faith into another dimension. The speed of light is an enormous number —to square it is unfathomable. The Word of God is magnanimous— the power released when you speak it is not just doubling it but squaring it! Okay, that blows your mind.

E = (energy) the supernatural power of God to change
something
M = (mass) object of your faith
C = (constant) the Word of God
2 = (squared) God's Word in your mouth!

Jesus taught His disciples this over and over in the gospels. In Mark 11:23 and Matthew 17:20, He tells them to speak to their mountain (seen facts) in faith to manifest the promise (unseen truth).

I say to you, if you have faith as a mustard seed, you will say to this mountain, 'Move from here to there,' and it will move; and nothing will be impossible for you. (Matt. 17:20)

So Jesus answered and said to them, "Have faith in God. For assuredly, I say to you, whoever says to this mountain, 'Be removed and be cast into the sea,' and does not doubt in his heart, but believes that those things he says will be done, he will have whatever he says. Therefore I say to you, whatever things you ask when you pray, believe that you receive them, and you will have them.
(Mark 11:22–24)

Do you spend more time talking ABOUT the mountain or TO the mountain? We cry and complain about our problems and even compare them to other people's. But Jesus said to speak TO our problem (FACTS) about how BIG our God is!

We speak to our mountain about how BIG our God is (TRUTH), not cry to God about how big our mountain is (FACTS). Instead of telling God how big my mountain is, I need to tell my mountain how BIG my God is!

BETTING YOUR LIFE ON UNSEEN REALITIES

God called Abraham out of the tent of his facts. The fact was he was old. Sarah was old. It's hilarious and embarrassing for a one-hundred-year-old man to even dream of having a baby. God took him for a walk and told him to look up from his facts to the stars above. Those stars were a prophetic picture of the nation Abraham would father. The facts were seen, but Abraham bet this life on the unseen reality of God's Word to him. It didn't make sense. It required a new set of faith eyes to see through the SEEN BARRIER into the SPIRIT.

Someone once asked me, "Are you one of those faith preachers?" Trying to discern what they were really asking, I said, "What other kind is there? Those who preach doubt and unbelief?" Hebrews 11:6 says that without faith it is impossible to please God, not because He's mean, but because He's GOOD. It pleases God to give us all the promises He has purchased for us in Christ.

 Remember, the facts can't change the truth, but the truth can change the facts!"

Is your confidence resting in the Facts or the Truth? It takes no faith to believe in the facts. They are seen, heard, and felt. They surround you and try to overwhelm you. BUT, there is a greater reality of God's truth that takes FAITH to step into. I love how Clarence Jordan translates Hebrews 11:1: *"Now faith is the turning of dreams into deeds; it's betting your life on unseen realities."* [6]

Now get this, the Scripture says it was credited to Abraham as righteousness when he **believed,** not when he **received!** We're not responsible to manifest the promise—that's God's part in His timing and His way. It is our part to embrace the truth, believe His Word is true, and exalt it over the facts by speaking, declaring, and acting in it. The by-product of our faith is God's work, not mine. Let that sink in for a minute. I am not responsible for the results of my faith, I am responsible to believe.

. . .

What Is Faith?

- Seeing the Unseen
- Turning Dreams into Deeds
- Betting Your Life on Unseen Realities

Abraham's righteousness was in his believing, not in producing a son. Just because what you are believing for hasn't manifested doesn't mean you have no faith. The producing is God's; the believing is mine. My faith can only respond to what grace has already provided. My responsibility is my ability to respond. Faith is my ability to respond to God's grace. Remember, the facts can't change the truth, but the truth can change the facts!

> *Against all hope, Abraham in hope believed and so became the father of many nations, just as it had been said to him, "So shall your offspring be." Without weakening in his faith, he faced the fact that his body was as good as dead—since he was about a hundred years old—and that Sarah's womb was also dead. Yet he did not waver through unbelief regarding the promise of God, but was strengthened in his faith and gave glory to God, being fully persuaded that God had power to do what he had promised. This is why "it was credited to him as righteousness." The words "it was credited to him" were written not for him alone, but also for us, to whom God will credit righteousness—for us who believe in him who raised Jesus our Lord from the dead. (Rom. 4:18–24, NIV, emphasis added)*

The *King James* says Abraham staggered not at the promise in verse 20 ("wavered" in NKJV), but was strengthened in his faith. He "faced the fact" that his body needed a miracle (v. 19) without weakening in his faith. We're not burying our head in the sand about our present circumstance, we're just believing there's a greater vision.

Habakkuk 2:2 says to "write the vision and make it plain . . . that he may run that reads it." We embrace the truth when we see and speak the greater unseen promise and run with it.

Habakkuk continues to encourage us in verse 3, "For the vision is yet for an appointed time; but at the end IT WILL SPEAK, and it will not lie." Abraham spoke the vision as it tarried for years until one day the vision spoke! Isaac spoke for himself—the vision manifested. We speak the vision until one day the vision speaks for itself!

Know the Truth

We had the wonderful privilege of living in the beautiful city of Lincoln in rural England for almost two years. Lincoln has one of the greatest cathedrals in England as well as a magnificent castle. One day while we were touring the castle with friends, the guide explained why the turrets are round instead of square. He said that originally they were square, but they found that when opposing armies attacked the castle walls, they hit them with huge battering rams, crumbling them and making the fortress penetrable.

Eventually, they learned that if they rounded these turrets, the force of the battering ram would reinforce the strength of the defense rather than weaken it. The Lord began to speak to me immediately about a principle in 2 Corinthians 10. Many people hear a truth one time, attempt to attack the fortress of thought in their mind, and when the wall does not immediately fall down, it actually strengthens the argument against the truth.

For example, someone gets a revelation about giving one big offering and after they give, immediately their finances get worse. Then, they think, *See, that giving stuff doesn't work at all!* Another person hears "a truth" about healing and prays for a sick friend, and they get worse! The conclusion is that healing is not for everyone. We are more intimate with the facts than the truth.

And you shall know the truth, and the truth shall make you free.
(John 8:32)

We read John 8:32 and think, *If I hear the truth, then that truth will instantly set me free.* However, there are many different words in Greek for the word "know." In English, we use "know" to mean different things. I meet someone one time, and I say, "I know them." If you ask me, "Do you know that person?" I would say, "Yes," but what I mean is "I've met them."

The word "know" in John 8:32 does not mean to simply be introduced to someone or something. It means "to be intimately acquainted with," and it is progressive in nature. I'm set free by the Word of God—the TRUTH—with which I become intimately acquainted. As I handle the truth, analyze it, look at it, and embrace it, then I become intimately acquainted with it. It becomes part of me. I become one with it, and the truth begins to make me freer and freer. *The Passion Translation* notes put it this way, "Truth must be embraced and worked out through the divine process of spiritual maturity. The Greek word for 'truth' is reality. To embrace the reality of Christ brings more freedom into your life."

The enemy's plan is to get us to *ginosko* (be more intimately acquainted with) the facts rather than the truth. I might have heard a truth and say, "I know that," but the question is, do I really *ginosko* it? Do I know (intimately acquainted with) the TRUTH or have I spent more time worrying about the FACTS or even the LIES of the enemy?

> *Am I more intimately acquainted with the TRUTH of God's promise or the temporary FACTS of my circumstance? Facts don't set you free.*

I KNOW THAT

Ralph Hagemeier, my missionary friend I mentioned earlier, preached a message over twenty-five years ago that still resonates in my heart. His text was Psalm 139:14: *"I will praise You, for I am fearfully and wonderfully made; marvelous are Your works, and **THAT** my soul knows very well."*

In his message, Ralph encouraged us that . . .

We may not know HOW
. . . How will it all work out and be okay?
We may not know WHEN
. . . Oh, Lord, when will you deliver me from this?
We may not know WHERE . . .
Where will the provision come from?
We may not even know WHY . . .
Why is this happening, Lord? I don't understand.

But, we can know THAT!

I know THAT—His truth. He loves me and made me for a purpose. I know THAT greater is He that is in me than He that is in the world. I know THAT all things work together for good to those who love God and are called according to His purpose! I am His, and *that I know well.* Life is a mystery, and we may never know the how, when, where, and why, but peace comes in knowing *that!*

. . .

LIVING IN LIGHT OF ETERNITY

In Chapter 1 we saw how Chuck Yeager broke the sound barrier, but in Christ we are called to break the *seen* barrier. As we continue to exegete 2 Corinthians chapter 4, we come to verses 16–18.

> *Therefore we do not lose heart. Even though our outward man is perishing, yet the inward man is being renewed day by day. For our light affliction, which is but for a moment, is working for us a far more exceeding and eternal weight of glory....*
> (2 Cor. 4:16–17)

The facts: Our outward man is perishing (and it's not pretty).
The truth: Our inward man is renewed daily.
The facts: I'm being afflicted (and it hurts).
The truth: The affliction is temporary and it is working for me an eternal weight of glory!

> *While we do not look at the things which are seen, but at the things which are not seen. For the things which are seen are temporary, but the things which are not seen are eternal.* (2 Cor. 4:18 NKJV)

While we look, breaking through the barrier of all the FACTS that we face and feel, our FOCUS is on unseen realities of TRUTH!

A few years ago, I was enjoying a meal with my family before boarding a plane to minister in Pennsylvania. Suddenly, it was as if a curtain closed on my eyesight in my left eye. I was very concerned, but I needed to catch the flight. The next day I learned my retina had detached. I sat in an ophthalmologist's office, and he asked me the famous question, "Can you tell me what you see on the chart?" He covered my right eye, and I looked through my ailing left eye.

Nothing!

I gasped, realizing I only saw a broken and distorted image. I told the doctor, "I can't even see the big E. I know it should be there, but I can't make it out." I knew what I *should* be seeing, but all I could see looked like shattered glass. Through a series of failed surgeries, the Lord led me on a journey to find my vision again. It was uncanny how the attack on my natural sight reflected an attack on my spiritual sight.

Just like the doctor asked, "What do you see in front of you?" the Lord began asking me, "What do you see?" At this time, my son, Cody, was a teenager, and I picked him up from football practice. Of course, he was starving (exaggeration intended), so we stopped for a hamburger on the way home. He left the raw onions off the burger and tossed them in the trash. I asked him to please take out the bag with the raw onions from my brand-new truck. I hate the nasty smell raw onions leave behind. Of course, my son forgot the bag with the onions, leaving them in my truck overnight. When I opened the door, the smell of onions nearly catapulted me backward to the driveway! I fumed at the facts, until God shifted my vision.

FACT: My truck smelled like an onion farm because my son forgot to take his trash with him.

TRUTH: This situation is temporary, but the relationship with my son is eternal. I can teach my son without fretting over the facts.

Look for the BIG E! Ecclesiastes 3:11 says, *"He has made everything beautiful in its time. Also He has put eternity in their hearts . . . ."* That ETERNITY is the BIG E! Focus on that, and everything else will fall into place. We've come so far from the days of just longing for a "cabin in the corner of glory." (Yes, that was a real song.) Thank God! We are moving from the white-knuckle theology that says just hold on until Jesus comes! There is a realm more real than our five senses. It's more than the "pie in the sky, in the sweet by and by"; it's a dimension God invites us to manifest here in the nasty now and now. Our life on earth should be a flow from heaven to earth. Just like Jacob saw a ladder from heaven with angels ascending and descending and said, "Surely the Lord was in this place and I was not unaware!"

I pray for a divine Lasik surgery to sharpen our focus on the Big E—things that matter for ETERNITY, things like people, relationships, obedience, prayers, and giving. These are all eternal. Let us ask the question, will this FACT even matter in ten days, ten months, ten years, in eternity?

Today, the FACT is that I'm legally blind in my left eye. The TRUTH is that God is bigger than this handicap and I'm believing for the manifestation of my healing to come; until it does, God has strengthened my right eye to compensate. He will make all things beautiful in the light of eternity.

So no wonder we don't give up. For even though our outer person gradually wears out, our inner being is renewed every single day. We view our slight, short-lived troubles in the light of eternity. We see our difficulties as the substance that produces for us an eternal, weighty glory far beyond all comparison, because we don't focus our attention on what is seen but on what is unseen. For what is seen is temporary, but the unseen realm is eternal. (2 Cor. 4:16–18 TPT)

6

BEYOND YOU

> *And he died for all, that those who live should no longer live*
> *for themselves but for him who died for them and was*
> *raised again."*
> —2 Cor. 5:15 NIV

In 1999, the world anticipated the millennial rollover with great trepidation. How would our computer systems respond to the new decade of 2000? People bought Y2K survival kits, hid their money, and wondered if the world as we knew it would end. The last thing people wanted was to travel overseas. Some people feared that planes might fall from the sky due to computer failures. This created a huge opportunity for me—a divine appointment! I purchased a round-trip ticket to London for $99 to fly January 2, 2000. Yes, you heard me—$99!

We enjoyed the wisdom and friendship of Norman and Grace Barnes, the founders of the United Kingdom-based mission organization Links International. Our Azle church hosted teams from

England led by the Barneses, and a unique bond formed. Many people prophesied over me how my destiny was linked to England. At this point I had ministered in Honduras, Mexico, Romania, and across Africa many times, but England truly was a whole new world —or new *old world?*

A few years before this, our spiritual father and mother, B. B. and Velma Hankins, laid hands on Kris and me and prayed a special prayer of blessing and anointing for missions to take their heart beyond where they had gone. They prayed, "Don't be afraid of their faces. It's the anointing to go beyond your own abilities, a stronger anointing than ever before. Beyond your own wisdom, beyond your own strength, beyond your own abilities." I thought, *Okay, Lord, I'm sensing a theme with the word "beyond" here.*

> *So, for $99, I packed my bag bound for the United Kingdom to see what God would do."*

I served with Paul and Perrianne Brownback in Azle, Texas, for thirteen years, and we all sensed the winds had shifted and it was time for us to launch out full time into mission work. So, for $99, I packed my bag bound for the United Kingdom to see what God would do.

BIRTH OF BEYOND THESE SHORES

"Beyond these shores—that sounds like your vision to me," my new friend, Clive Price, said as I appreciated the hospitality of his cottage in Littlehampton, England. He listened to my vision to inspire people in living for something beyond themselves and reach nations by empowering leaders and equipping churches around the world. It made little sense. How could a small-town, no-name nobody launch a worldwide ministry to reach nations?

As I divulged my vision to launch into the deep unknown, Clive skillfully captured my imagination with Celtic Christians who had desired the same thing. He shared epic stories of St. Brendan's voyages in a small leather and wood boat, blown by the winds of the Holy Spirit. The ancient Irish monk, known as St. Brendan the Navigator, sailed into the great unknown and some say discovered North America or at least inspired Christopher Columbus's later New World voyages. Clive played a song by one of his favorite Celtic bands, Iona, called "Beyond These Shores," which symbolized Brendan's bold sea faith. The words grabbed my heart as a reflection of God's call for me to leave all I had known as well.

Beyond these shores, Into the darkness
Beyond these shores,
This boat may sail
And if this is the way,
Then there will be
A path across this sea and if I sail beyond,
The farthest ocean
Or lose myself in depths below, wherever I may go
Your love surrounds me, For you have been before
Beyond these shores
—Iona, "Beyond These Shores"[1]

It was an epic moment of destiny, and Beyond These Shores Missions Network came to life in the living room of a caring friend on the south shore of England. We already had the legal organization of Duane White Ministries, but we desired to found a mission network that wasn't about me, but beyond me. Okay, I think Beyond These Shores sums it up beautifully.

THE PRAYER OF ST. BRENDAN
"Help me to journey beyond the familiar and into the unknown.
Give me the faith to leave old ways
and break fresh ground with You.
Christ of the mysteries, I trust You to be stronger than each storm
within me. I will trust in the darkness and know that my times,
even now, are in Your hand.
Tune my spirit to the music of heaven,
and somehow, make my obedience count for You."
AMEN.

I spent time with my British friend Rich Hubbard, whom I met in Burundi and who would later become one of the first board members of Beyond These Shores. He prayed and encouraged me as we both shared a passion for world missions. I then traveled four hours up to Lincoln, England, where Kate Barker had invited me to meet her pastor, Pete Atkins, and the leader of Pete's network, Pastor Stuart Bell. They invited me to a house group meeting in their conservatory and asked if I wanted to share what I saw God doing around the world, then I prayed for people and sensed God's presence there in such a special way.

As Bishop Tony Miller always says, *"Big doors swing on little hinges."* Doors started opening into the nation of England. It was favor that didn't make sense, except it was God's huper anointing. We were walking in the FOG—the Favor of God! One relationship led to another, and before we knew it, Kris and I sold our house and most of our belongings and moved our family to Lincoln, England. We were committed to stay for six months, but we both felt in our hearts that it would probably be longer.

We stayed for almost two years, and God used this time to establish the work of Beyond These Shores beyond the United States. Stories abound of how God connected us in huper ways beyond what I could have ever arranged in my own strength.

My motto has become "I love it when my friends meet my friends," and it has been an honor to connect people for God's kingdom work. Because of those connections, marriages, many joint teams, and micro-finance projects materialized. Additionally, Beyond These Shores has taken thousands of people on short-term mission trips, worked in over fifty nations, and hosted multitudes of pastors and leaders conferences; and I have personally spoken to over 125,000 pastors and leaders face to face. Totally beyond me!

Not for Yourself but the Whole World

A dear friend, Perrianne Brownback, told me of a BBC documentary she watched about the world-renowned band The Beatles. Two of the band members, legendary Paul McCartney and George Harrison, attended school at the Liverpool Institute for Boys. As the boys walked the halls every day, they read the school motto inscribed in Latin, *"Non Nobis Solum Sed Toti Mundo Nati."* Translated, the motto means, "Not for ourselves alone, but for the whole world were we born."

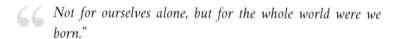 *Not for ourselves alone, but for the whole world were we born."*

The phrase originated from a work of Cicero that suggests that we were not born for ourselves but for our country and friends who have a share in us. No doubt those words fueled those two young men, and no matter what you think of their music, they undoubtedly changed the world. Decades later, Paul McCartney questioned if he still believed in the motto.

McCartney's autobiographical opera, *Liverpool Oratorio*, symbolizes his struggle. "But I can say that looking back the most important thing I found was sagging off! Not for the whole world, but for yourself were you born" ("Movement II – School").[2]

I'm not sure where McCartney stands today with his higher call beyond himself, but it poignantly portrays the struggle of man. Do I serve myself or lay down my life and serve a bigger kingdom beyond me? What if the kingdom really is depending on my obedience? Does my life have a share in someone else's? What if someone is waiting on me . . . Beyond These Shores? Beyond my street? Beyond my politics? Beyond my culture? Beyond my race? Beyond my age? Beyond what I've known? What if God's favor isn't for you alone but for those who will follow you?

BEYOND RACIAL ROPES

Evangelist Billy Graham lived a bold life beyond himself. In the summer of 1957, he pioneered one of the greatest revivals of our time in New York City and called for a spiritual revolution crossing racial boundaries. Disappointed in the low turnout of African Americans in the first weeks of his landmark crusade in Madison Square Garden, Graham enlisted the help of Rev. Howard Jones. He invited him to be the first black pastor to serve with his team as an evangelist. Jones writes in his autobiography that white pastors actually moved to the other side of the stage to avoid sitting by him and refused to pray in his vicinity.

It's hard for us to imagine this injustice today, but in 1957 it was a reality. Letters to Graham flooded his ministry, threatening a withholding of support if he continued to invite minorities onto his evangelistic team. Jones, whose grandmother was born a slave in Virginia, would later become the first black evangelist sent from the United States to hold revivals in Africa. Jones said, *"The gospel has always transcended whatever racial or cultural boundaries we've constructed to limit it."*

Pastor Jones continued to work with Graham for forty years. Although grateful for the doors Dr. Graham opened for him, he also expressed the extreme pressure of his calling by saying, "It is an honor to overcome a barrier that has long kept blacks on an unequal footing with whites. But, along with the outer triumph, there is an inner ache—an angst—of having to live with the often unfriendly fallout of going where no black man has ever gone before." [3]

> *The gospel has always transcended whatever racial or cultural boundaries we've constructed to limit it."*
>
> - HOWARD JONES

No doubt pioneering has a price. The sacrifice is great, but the reward exceeds it. Fed up with the ropes that segregated races in the Madison Square Garden auditorium, Graham asked an usher to remove them. The usher refused, so Graham marched down and removed the ropes himself. Revolutionary. Risking his earthly support, but backed by his greater heavenly support, Graham transcended the boundaries the American church had known in that season. During the NYC crusade, Graham invited a twenty-eight-year-old Dr. Martin Luther King Jr. to the stage to pray.

"And in these days of emotional tension—when the problems of the world are gigantic in extent and chaotic in detail—give us penetrating vision, broad understanding, power of endurance, and abiding faith, and save us from the paralysis of crippling fear.
And O God, we ask Thee to help us to work

with renewed vigor for a warless world and for a brotherhood that
transcends race or color."[4]
(Prayer by Dr. Martin Luther King Jr., July 18, 1957,
Madison Square Garden Crusade)

As Graham shared the stage, he served future disciples who had a share in his obedience. In God's kingdom, others have a "share" in your obedience. Someone had to go first. After sixteen weeks, the final count: Almost two million people (all races) freely attended the crusade and over 56,000 committed their lives to Christ, according to the Billy Graham archives. [5]

This story inspires us with the boldness Graham and Jones displayed in their day, but it's our turn now. These *huper* men have received their reward now in heaven. They ran their race. It's our time to lay down our lives, to make a way for others. What boundaries are you called to cross to make a way for someone else's victory today?

BEYOND NORMAL

If you struggled as a kid for standing out or were bullied for being different, then you understand the temptation to just blend in, just be normal like everyone else, to fade away into obscurity. We define normal as conforming to a standard, usual, typical or expected. Everyone wants to be an extraordinary person, but few realize how that's not normal! To be an "extra" ordinary person, be willing to leave the limits of ordinary. Ordinary is comfortable. It's safe there on the shore with the crowd. Extra ordinary is beyond your comfort zone.

David Livingstone, one of my heroes, heard the words of a veteran missionary and his future father-in-law, Robert Moffat, in

1836: "I have sometimes seen, in the morning sun, the smoke of a thousand villages where no one has ever heard the name of Christ." These words stirred a passion in young David that never relented and sent him into his African adventure. Upon arriving, Livingstone grew disappointed with the other missionaries who remained safely on the shores, drinking tea and immersed in gossip and politics. He had not come all that way to stay safe and ordinary on the shore, so he ventured into the interior of the darkest parts of Africa.

And although I see few results, future missionaries will see conversions following every sermon. May they not forget the pioneers who worked in the thick gloom with few rays to cheer, except such as flow from faith in the precious promises of God's Word. - David Livingstone

I've led many mission teams connecting through London and taken them to Westminster Abbey to see Livingstone's gravestone. Standing there in the Nave, I challenge the team to continue Livingstone's legacy. Legend says that Livingstone proclaimed his body might belong to the Queen but his heart belonged to Africa. He died kneeling in prayer by his bed, and his faithful attendants removed his heart and buried it under an mpundu tree in present day Zambia (in the heart of Africa) to honor his declaration.

Today, Livingstone's bones are buried in a grave in Westminster Abbey, but his heart is still buried in Africa. What belongs to your heart? There may be circumstances beyond your control that lay claim to your life, but YOU choose what your heart belongs to! Where will your heart be buried?

Parts of Africa look at history as B.L. and A.L. (Before Livingstone and After Livingstone) because of his discoveries and connections. I've toured the Livingstone Museum in Blantyre, Scotland, and seen his handwritten journals and drawings. I've seen the doctor's bag he carried into the interior of Africa where no white man had ever journeyed and where lions mauled him. I've seen the movie projector he used to show Jesus films to whoever would watch.

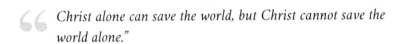

> *Christ alone can save the world, but Christ cannot save the world alone."*
>
> *— DAVID LIVINGSTONE*

People may criticize Livingstone's methods, and we can learn much from his regrets; but one thing's for certain—HE WAS NOT NORMAL! He said himself, "I have found that I have no unusual endowments of intellect, but this day I resolve that I will be an uncommon Christian." Normal people make history, but history makers are never normal people. God calls ordinary, average people to do extraordinary things for Him.

It's Our Turn Now

Not all are called to Nigeria, Nepal, or North Korea, but maybe you're called to your neighbor. The Great Commission charges us to go into all the world, but YOUR world may be your child's school, your workplace, and your neighborhood. Under the broad umbrella of Great Commission (Matt. 28:19–20) are "sub-missions"—unique assignments under the main mission. That's really what "submission" is: coming under the mission. God has given each of us a grace or empowerment for our own unique contribution to advance the cause of Christ.

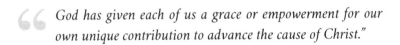

> *God has given each of us a grace or empowerment for our own unique contribution to advance the cause of Christ."*

Just as the military might have an overarching mission to take back a territory, each branch is commissioned for its unique part in the battle. Thinking old school for a minute, imagine if an infantry soldier accidentally joined the cavalry? He'd be behind everyone else and feel like he's missing something, which he would be—he needs a horse! But, what if a cavalry soldier joined the infantry? Those soldiers would look at him and say, "Man, get off your high horse! Who do you think you are, always running ahead?" This may be a silly example, but it's true in the kingdom of God.

God fashioned us uniquely for the place He's called us to serve. We usually only think of grace as "saving grace," but in the New Testament the Greek word for grace, *charis*, also means favor and empowerment for service. Romans 12 exhorts us to serve in the grace given us.

> *God's marvelous grace imparts to each one of us varying gifts and ministries that are uniquely ours* . . . . (Rom. 12:6 TPT)

Maybe you have a special *grace* for athletics to glorify God in the world in sports, or a *grace* for teaching to train the next generation, or a *grace* to be an entrepreneur or start a kingdom business, or a *grace* to sing and write songs, or a *grace* to preach and declare God's Word.

We are all called to display the gospel of Christ in a unique, uncommon, extraordinary way that displays the glory of God! We'll never be fulfilled striving to live in someone else's grace or anointing. That's like trying to ride your horse in the infantry. We'll also be frustrated living below our calling. Imagine if Livingstone had stayed on the African shore drinking tea? Even with lions and malaria, obedience is better than settling for the lowest common denominator of public opinion. At the same time, we will be frustrated striving beyond our anointing. There's no HUPER strength for doing God's will our way.

He graces us for what HE's prepared for us, not what we've called for or prepared for ourselves. Stop comparing yourself to others, and run in your lane. He's made us living stones—not bricks! God calls us to unity, not uniformity. You're not normal. You're peculiar! There is grace for your race when you're in pace with God's HUPER anointing for your unique destiny. That's the race that Hebrews 12 tells us to run with endurance that's "set" before us. Each of us has a different race under His great commission.

Therefore we also, since we are surrounded by so great a cloud of witnesses, let us lay aside every weight, and the sin which so easily ensnares us, and let us run with endurance the race that is set before us . . . . (Heb. 12:1 NKJV)

David Livingstone, Billy Graham, and Howard Jones joined the great cloud of witnesses. They passed the baton and cheer us on as we run our leg. We stand on the shoulders of great men and women who pioneered before us, but it's our turn now. It's our responsibility to build on the breakthroughs of our fathers and mothers in the faith and make their struggle continue to bear fruit. Imagine someday shaking the hand of these heroes in heaven. Do you want to tell them you lived a "normal" Christian life?

Do you want to tell Howard Jones that people stopped trying to break down prejudice and put the ropes back up? Do you want to explain to Billy Graham how the entertainment options on Netflix and YouTube were just too mesmerizing and we stopped doing crusades and revivals? Do you want to tell David Livingstone we stopped believing in missions because the "campfires" are better left alone? Do we tell Jesus we failed the great commission because it didn't seem safe, it didn't fit into our busy schedule, or it might upset someone if not politically correct? No, by God's grace, we pray that each generation will run *their* race and the kingdom will continually advance exceedingly beyond us! It's our turn now. Grab the baton and run your race!

"Until you have given up yourself to Him you will not have a real self. Sameness is to be found most among 'normal' men, not among those who surrender to Christ. How monotonously alike all the great tyrants and conquerors have been: how gloriously different are the saints."
(C. S. Lewis, *Mere Christianity*)

[PART 2]

HUPER LIVING

It's one thing to quote Scriptures on the sofa, but another to live them out on the front lines. In the next chapters, we'll discuss how to apply His HUPER power in different areas of life.

> *"Now to Him who is able to do exceedingly abundantly, above all that we ask or think, according to the power that works in us."*
> (Eph. 3:20)

The *New American Standard* version says, "Who is able to do far more abundantly beyond all that we ask. . . . " I like that word "beyond." Beyond what? Beyond me! *Beyond my abilities and natural limitations.* God loves to go beyond all that we could ever dream of.

The three Greek words here for exceedingly, abundantly, and beyond (or above) gave me a picture of myself that has changed my life. First, let's look at the word "abundantly." The Greek word is *perissōs*, which means "to go beyond a particular measure or boundary."

Abundantly (perissōs) = beyond measure, extraordinary, superior, super added [1]

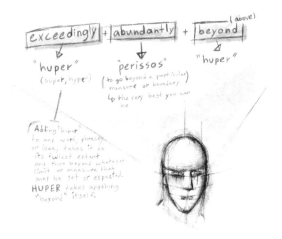

It means "full in stature, pre-eminent, supreme." So, in your life, it would mean, "the very best you can be in every area of your life." That's the nature of God in us—to make us the best we could ever dream of being. For some, that would be a major improvement—to just be the best they could be with their God-given talents and intellect. However, that is not what Paul was saying here. He wasn't saying, "YOU do your best to improve yourself, and that will be good enough. You be all YOU can be, and God will be happy." No, he doesn't leave the word *perissos* alone but takes it a step further. He didn't say God is able to do just "abundantly." He says God does EXCEEDINGLY abundantly!

Exceedingly *(huper)* = *over, beyond, more than* [2]

The word "exceedingly" is the awesome Greek prefix *"huper."* It sounds like "super" but with an "h." In English, it is like the word "hyper." Adding huper to any word, phrase, or idea takes it to its fullest extent and then beyond whatever limit or measure that may be set or expected. Huper takes anything beyond itself. It's like our word "hyperbole."

Paul is stressing this point here. He says God has put the power to work in each of us to be and do the very best we can be and do. But, He doesn't stop there. He adds more on top of that and more on top of that.

Above/Beyond *(huper)* = *over, beyond, more than* [3]

In the Greek it would read, *"huper perissos huper."* That doesn't make sense in English, so the translators had to give it different words. But can you see the emphasis God is trying to make? He takes the very, very best you can be and then adds HIS supernatural strength on top of that, but just so everyone knows His glory He adds more on top of that! He has provided "huper anointing." It is like the motto of Buzz Lightyear from the movie *Toy Story*: "To infinity and BEYOND!"

God desires to take very normal, average, ordinary people and do extraordinary, supernatural things through them. When other people look at them, they say, "Wow! That can't be that person. That must be God!"

God can do anything, you know—far more than you could ever imagine or guess or request in your wildest dreams! He does it not by pushing us around but by working within us, his Spirit deeply and gently within us. (Eph. 3:20 MSG)

Never doubt God's mighty power to work in you and accomplish all this. He will achieve infinitely more than your greatest request, your most unbelievable dream, and exceed your wildest imagination! He will outdo them all, for his miraculous power constantly energizes you. (Eph. 3:20 TPT)

To break barriers, we need power beyond our own strength. We're going to tap into God's supernatural, nothing's impossible, miracle-working HUPER power! You may be like Captain Chuck right now with no fanfare to your faith decision. No one's cheering your choice to push through to your breakthrough, but don't turn back, don't give up, because on the other side of your opposition, heaven is applauding and there's about to be a big BOOM into another dimension!

God has privileged us in Christ Jesus to live above the ordinary human plane of life. Those who want to be ordinary and live on a lower plane can do so, but as for me, I will not.

- SMITH WIGGLESWORTH

7

HUPER HOME: CONNECTION OVER PERFECTION

> *They will restore ruins from long ago and rebuild what was long devastated. . . ."*
> —Isa. 61:4 TPT

BROKEN HOMES BUILD barriers in your heart, making you question your identity and where you really belong. I'm thankful God sent a surrogate father to me who changed my life—my uncle John White. My dad's younger brother, he was one of the strongest men I have ever known. There's no horse he couldn't ride or thing he couldn't do, although he might have to go at it a different way. Polio crippled John from birth, and he wore metal braces on his left leg and drug his right leg behind him when he walked.

John had a tough and rugged exterior, but he also had a tender heart when you got through his thick skin. He played the guitar and loved to worship the Lord. I owe him an immense debt of gratitude. He took a lazy boy who was scared of his own shadow, who wasn't good at anything but eating potato chips and watching reruns on

TV, and gave him confidence and a place to belong. He taught me how to train and trade horses. He made me a man. I earned good money trading horses, but I knew I was called to preach and reach nations, so the time came when I had to step out in faith and believe God for the money to go to Bible college. God used my grandfather's new wife to provide the first big tuition installment, and I sold everything and surrendered to God's plan.

God planted me in a church in Azle, Texas, led by Pastors Paul and Perrianne Brownback. I served there as I studied at Christ for the Nations Institute. Everyone said I needed to find a job at a larger church in the Dallas metroplex, but I knew God had planted me in Azle. I always say if you cut me, I bleed missions and the local church. I wasn't leaving the church God called me to, so He would have to send a wife to me.

At the time, I served as a children's pastor on staff and also volunteered in youth ministry. One ordinary night as I welcomed youth into the service, I greeted a new girl, Kris Trammell. We became great friends, more like a big brother and sister. I mentored her in children's ministry and became good friends with her family, especially her dad, who shared my love of horses.

I was dedicated and driven to what God was doing and not interested in dating. God would just have to show me my wife—I didn't have time to waste on dates and wrong people. One night after church, I was hanging out at my pastor's house and Perrianne said, "What do you think about Kris Trammell?" I said, "What do you mean, what do I think? I think she's five and a half years younger, and she's like my little sister." Perrianne added, "Well, I think maybe you ought to pray about that a little more." I had never *imagined* Kris as my wife, but God revealed it by His Spirit . . . and my pastors.

Unknown to me, at the exact same time, God was speaking to Kris that I was her husband. She swore her dad to secrecy never to tell anyone, not knowing that God had already told him I would be his son-in-law. After a crazy chain of events, I asked Kris out on our first date. I told her dad I wasn't interested in dating, I wanted to marry her. We had the blessing of our pastors, our parents, and God. Now all I needed was a huper proposal.

Well, if you ask Kris, it wasn't very huper. It was more like an altar call. Sitting at the casual home-cooking restaurant eating hamburgers, I tested her, saying, "Kris, you need to count the cost. You know I'm called to preach to the world and serve the church. You know it's not going to be easy. People aren't always going to like you. It's not a walk in the park. Are you sure you're called to do this?" Pretty romantic, huh?

Well, Kris said yes and jokes that I should have received an offering after that big altar call. On March 16, 1991, she walked down the aisle to begin our covenant to the song "Just as I Am." We thought that was very fitting. We came into our covenant just like we came into salvation, just as we are—broken clay jars trusting the treasure within us.

BEYOND US

We started our lives together trusting God to provide way beyond our paychecks. I didn't make a lot from the church, and Kris made a small salary from her job in a clothing store. We didn't have much within ourselves, but we were committed to be good stewards of what we had. Miraculous provision rained in beyond us. We had a very small wedding budget and no honeymoon budget.

My mom worked for an airline at the time and frantically called me one day, saying, "Do you want to go to Florida for your honeymoon?" "Of course, but how much?" I answered. "Well, there's a mistake in the computer. Right now it's $75 instead of $750, and they have to honor it for a few hours. Do you want it?" We had tickets, but what about hotel and a car and things to do? We stumbled into a timeshare proposal that offered us a cheap hotel and Disney tickets to tour the timeshare. (I may have been speaking "by faith" to qualify to view it on my salary!) Uncle John paid for our rental car, and we were headed to Disney World!

As we walked through Epcot's World Showcase, we dreamed of the nations God had called us to reach. Impossible in ourselves. Possible with God. On our twenty-fifth wedding anniversary, we renewed our vows with our kids in Florida and walked through the World Showcase again, this time praising God because we had actually ministered in almost every country. HUPER.

Someone told us about an abandoned trailer house that we could buy and move for a small fee. Dead ants filled it, and the place needed new paint and carpet. But my wife has an eye for potential and isn't scared of hard work. That disgusting mobile home became our beautiful newlywed cottage. It was actually the beginning of house flips and renovations that we'd continue to do throughout our marriage and God would use as provision. Never despise the day of small beginnings. He finds you just as you are, but He never leaves you where He finds you!

Forgiveness Enlarges the Future

God did big things in our marriage as we learned how to sort through the baggage each of us unknowingly brought into our new life together. I started noticing the real root behind things that triggered me in our relationship. Kris would innocently say, "I'll just have my dad fix it if you can't do it." She had no idea how those words triggered memories of rejection in me—as a young man, when I tried to help my dad fix things, he'd tell me to go away. So I never learned. This is just one example of how we both would unknowingly push each other's "hot buttons" linked to unresolved hurt.

Just a few months before our marriage, a guest minister who flowed strongly in the prophetic visited our church. During one night of ministry, he told me that every time my dad had missed a ballgame or important event in my life, God, my forever Father, had been there. He had never left me or forsaken me. God began a deep work of HUPER healing in me. He was always my Father. He was always proud of me. He would never leave or forsake me.

And you did not receive the "spirit of religious duty," leading you back into the fear of never being good enough. But you have received the "Spirit of full acceptance," enfolding you into the family of God. And you will never feel orphaned, for as he rises up within us, our spirits join him in saying the words of tender affection, "Beloved Father!" (Rom. 8:15 TPT)

As I received the love of my heavenly Father, my perspective on my earthly father changed. God wanted me to forgive him and let the past go. How can you forgive someone who doesn't deserve it or didn't even ask for it? My dad could never repay the debt of cheating on my mom and leaving us and giving his time and attention to his new family. He could never make up for that—the debt was too great for him to pay, but it wasn't too great for the cross to pay. No one deserves grace. It's an unearned free gift. I knew that God was asking me to extend that free gift of grace to my dad. I didn't have enough love or strength to forgive in my own human heart, but beyond myself there was huper grace from the heart of God.

"Forgiveness does not change the past, but it does enlarge the future." -Paul Boose

One afternoon I called him. He lived nine hours away, and I didn't see him often. This time was different than any time before. This time I came to the relationship with a full heart, not an empty one begging for something he couldn't give. My heart was filled with acceptance from my heavenly Father, and I didn't need it from my dad. My identity as a son of God in Christ superseded my DNA as his biological son. I told him I honored him for being my dad and that I knew he was the best dad he knew how to be and I was glad that he was mine . . . fill in the blanks. My forgiveness released him of the expectations he could never fulfill, but somehow in the freedom, he began to be more present. That year, for the first time ever, he sent me a birthday card—it even had cash in it! Later, he told me how that phone call freed him from years of guilt and condemnation. It wiped the slate clean for us to start again.

It took time to refill the vaults in our relational bank, but we built a friendship that only God could create. I took him to England, where he heard me preach for the first time when I was thirty-four. (I had been preaching since I was twenty-one.) As my dad rode on a train peering out at the beautiful English countryside, he began to weep. He told me how proud he was of me and what an incredible preacher I was. He couldn't believe all he had seen and experienced. He said, "Man, if church had been like this when I was young, maybe things would've been a lot different. All I ever heard was what I couldn't do, not what all God could do in my life!"

My kids enjoyed a great relationship with my dad, their Grandpa Don. They never ate sour grapes of the past. God did a beautiful work in his heart, and my kids didn't recognize the person from the past; they only knew him surrounded by grace as their grandpa.

The people will no longer quote this proverb: 'The parents have eaten sour grapes, but their children's mouths pucker at the taste.'
(Jer. 31:29 NLT)

They have wonderful memories of my dad going to Africa and England with us, eating ice cream, making waffles for them, and feeling loved and special. Only God—HUPER! Forgiveness turned our bitter water sweet. My decision to forgive my dad and let go of trying to hold him accountable for what he owed me was the best decision I've ever made. It stopped a cycle, and it began rebuilding the ruins. Without the assurance and love from Father God, this restoration would never have happened.

HANDOUTS FROM HOME

We have been blessed with a special relationship with our friends and teachers, Dr. Graham and Marie Catto. Every year, they minister with us at our church, what we call, LTS or Life Transformation School, that they started some thirty-five years ago in South Africa. During this intensive two weeks, Dr. Graham shares that our family shapes most of who we are by the time we're five years old. He teaches that God designed families to give three important gifts for the foundation of the rest of our lives.

God Uses the Family to Give Us . . .

1. **Security:** (*protection, freedom from fear, anxiety and danger*)
   This gift is imparted and then received. Family gives us a sense of security and protection; this is why God gave us guidance for family in his Word. If we grow up without security, we have anxiety and emotional unsteadiness where if one thing changes or shifts, it causes the whole world to fall apart. Consistent and loving discipline

bestows security by building boundaries of safety and structure.

2. **Belonging:** *(fitting in and meshing within a close relationship)* This shows you that you're part of something bigger than yourself. I fit here. I'm accepted just because I'm a part. If this is not received, you are left with a longing and wayward wandering for who will accept you, or you will become competitive to prove you belong!

3. **Identity:** *(comes from Latin meaning "same as")* Identity tells you who you are, shapes a worldview, and attributes core values. When you identify with a family, you say, "I'm the same as them" and see yourself through their heritage.

You can see how God created the family to instill these important gifts into children to ensure their success. The only problem is that most homes in the United States could be considered dysfunctional, and, with the disintegration of the family, these important gifts are not being deposited. Psychologists agree that you can trace most addictive behavior to family life. We see the vicious cycles repeat over and over until our heads spin. How can fathers and mothers parent when they were never parented? How can you give something that you've never experienced yourself? We need breakthrough—a healing, a change that breaks free for a fresh start. A love that's higher and greater than the sins of our forefathers. A love that's beyond us. It's *huper*.

THE RUNWAY TO EPHESIANS 3:20

Let's look back at one of our main verses in Ephesians 3. Remember the promise in Ephesians 3:20?

*Now to Him who is able to do exceedingly abundantly above all
that we ask or think, according to the power that works in us.*

This promise sounds like healing from a dysfunctional childhood. It sounds like a new security, belonging, and identity with a greater power than I muster in myself and all my self-help mantras. Let's look at the verses that introduce our pivotal theme Scripture. Read Ephesians 3:14–19. Here it is in *The Passion Translation*, with the heading "Paul Prays for Love to Overflow."

*So I kneel humbly in awe before the Father of our Lord Jesus, the
Messiah, the perfect Father of every father and child in heaven and
on the earth. And I pray that he would unveil within you the
unlimited riches of his glory and favor until supernatural strength
floods your innermost being with his divine might and explosive
power.* **Then, by constantly using your faith, the life of Christ
will be released deep inside you, and the resting place of his love
will become the very source and root of your life.** *Then you will
be empowered to discover what every holy one experiences—the
great magnitude of the astonishing love of Christ in all its
dimensions. How deeply intimate and far-reaching is his love! How
enduring and inclusive it is! Endless love beyond measurement that
transcends our understanding—this extravagant love pours into
you until you are filled to overflowing with the fullness of God!*
(Eph. 3:14–19 TPT, emphasis added)

This revelation is the runway to the Ephesians 3:20 liftoff. It's the full-stop revelation alleviating cycles from repeating themselves. In Christ, I am now adopted into the family of God! I have SECURITY, granted the riches of His glory, BELONGING, filled with the fullness of God, and IDENTITY, given His name. Here it is in the *New King James Version*:

For this reason I bow my knees to the Father of our Lord Jesus
Christ, from whom the whole family in heaven and earth is named,
that He would grant you, according to the riches of His glory, to be
strengthened with might through His Spirit in the inner man, that
Christ may dwell in your hearts through faith; that you, being
rooted and grounded in love, may be able to comprehend with all
the saints what is the width and length and depth and height—to
know the love of Christ which passes knowledge; that you may be
filled with all the fullness of God. (Eph. 3:14–19)

Look at verse 19, "to know the love of Christ which passes
knowledge." The phrase translated "passes knowledge" is the
HUPER word *huperballo,* meaning "to throw over and beyond
again." His love for you is BEYOND anything you've ever known. It
can't be compared to anything you've ever experienced before. It is
HUPER. The runway is the Father's love! We now have takeoff into
Ephesians 3:20. "NOW to him who is able. . . ." Who is able? Our
Father!

PERFECT PARENTS

I didn't have a perfect father, but neither do my kids. At times I've
been too controlling and involved when I should have taken my
hands off. Sometimes I've been too absent when they needed me to
be present. I've messed up and failed them even when I didn't mean
to. My heart is always there to love and protect them, but I've realized (and my kids certainly have)—that I'm human. I'm *not* perfect.
In all the things that I promised myself, "When I'm a dad, I'll never .
. ." or "Someday when I have kids, I'll always . . . ." These verdicts are
judgments vowed in the light of my father's failures that boomerang
right back at me. Matthew chapter seven talks about these

boomerang judgments, but also encourages us that the grace we give will be given back to us!

> *Refuse to be a critic full of bias toward others, and judgment will not be passed on you. For you'll be judged by the same standard that you've used to judge others. The measurement you use on them will be used on you.* (Matt. 7:1–2 TPT)

The grace to forgive where it's not deserved, originates from the heart of our perfect heavenly father. Remember Ephesians 3:15, "The perfect Father of every father and child in heaven and on the earth (TPT)." The footnote in *The Passion Translation* this verse says, *"Translated from the Aramaic. It could also be translated as 'the perfect Father of every people group.' The Greek word for 'father' and the word for 'family' are quite similar, which indicates that every family finds its source in the Father."*[1] Every family finds its source or IDENTITY in the FATHER.

None of us have perfect fathers on earth. A few have had really good ones, but compared to the "endless love beyond measurement that transcends our understanding" (v. 18), they all pale in comparison because they were human, clay jars in the need of a Savior themselves. How we view our earthly father is the lens we see God the Father through until—IN CHRIST—we experience salvation and realize we are "born again" into God's family. We have HIS name, we belong to Him forever, we are "the same" (identity) as Him, and that security weeds out the need for petty comparison and competition.

IN CHRIST the imaginary link from our earthly father to God reconnects to our heavenly Father. We are linked to Him, and now we can see our earthly parents through HIS EYES—not the eyes of our hurt and past!

. . .

TURNED TO THE FATHER'S HEART

Pastors and leaders in Vietnam were extremely concerned that their sons and daughters were turning away from the Lord. They sacrificed their lives, survived prison and persecution, but now their children were more interested in the internet and could not understand the fervor of their parents' faith. The kids were connected to social media but were not connected to God or their families. Their parents knew how to survive persecution but struggled to show affection to and understanding of their children. As the church leaders voiced this problem, we ventured to hold a family camp that would "turn the hearts of the father to the children and the children back to their fathers." This has been one of the most fruitful things I've invested my ministry in.

Over the course of five years, I have returned every year to pour into these families. I've seen miraculous transformation. The young people who were rebellious and critical toward God have become church leaders because they experienced God's love—and love from their parents in a REAL way beyond religion and obligation. During a powerful prayer time where we ministered over national church leaders, I ran up and bear-hugged a very distinguished leader. I told him that is how his heavenly Father feels about him. He broke into a sobbing puddle saying that he had never received a hug from his dad before. That day he experienced the depths of God's love in a new way that healed his father's rejection. This encounter gave him a new mantle for real connection to future sons and daughters. It was a beautiful thing to witness!

'To turn the hearts of the fathers to the children,' and the disobedient to the wisdom of the just, to make ready a people prepared for the Lord." (Luke 1:17)

CONNECTION OVER PERFECTION

Every new parent hopes they won't make the same mistakes their parents made. Great intentions melt into repeated cycles of dysfunction without the power of the Holy Spirit to break them. Clay to clay. We're hopeless to break out of these strongholds, but the power working in us can set our families free. Huper families are not perfect. They are humbly being transformed and value connection over perfection.

> *Huper families are not perfect families. They are humbly being transformed and value connection over perfection!"*

Our goal is to display the love of God to our kids and connect them to the lavish love of their heavenly Father. We fight for their hearts first, not their habits. Just as the Father cares about our hearts more than just obeying religiously, hearts need connection; connection needs communication. Family communication is a "meeting of meaning" through discussion and shared perspective, not a one-way sermon. That's how God has always talked to man. He asked questions. He drew them in. He used parables and illustrations to ground things that are hard to grasp. He's a good Father.

Inevitably, times will arise when your home will not see things eye to eye. Kris and I will tell you that we don't always agree on everything. On most things our personalities are opposite like the North and South Pole. But the power of the Holy Spirit working (*huper*) in us fills the gaps when we're not connecting. It builds a bridge between us.

Huper homes rely on the power of the Holy Spirit to connect them and display God's love through them. It's messy, it's not easy, but you can rest in HIS strength. You're never going to be the perfect parent or spouse, so you might as well give up and start relying on His power to help you! It's your inheritance. It runs in the family—HIS family. Dysfunction may have run in your family, but IN CHRIST restoration runs in His!

I have to show you one last thing from Ephesians 3. We don't quote it often, but look at the end of the verse. It makes me want to do a happy dance!

To Him be glory in the church by Christ Jesus to all generations, forever and ever. Amen. (Eph. 3:21)

To ALL generations, forever. This a family thing, a generational blessing—to your children, and their children, and their children! There is hope for you and your household. The Father's love is available to restore you and create a HUPER home within you. Welcome to the family!

8

HUPER HEALING: MOVING YOUR MAT

I am the Lord who heals you."
—Exod. 15:26

AN ASSIGNMENT close to my heart has been my investment in the church of Vietnam. A dear friend, a former Vietnam war sniper, invited me to join him as he encouraged the persecuted believers there. Talk about a HUPER story. God took a man who had been tasked with killing people and commissioned him to heal them. When most men his age were retired and playing golf, he was braving the heat, enduring difficult travel situations, and risking a great deal to invest in this nation. I honor him.

He invited me and some fellow ministers to preach at a conference at an undisclosed location. I greatly anticipated the opportunity, but while I was ministering in Ireland, I grew violently ill. I barely boarded the flight from Dublin to London. While in transit at Heathrow Airport, my condition worsened. My friend and ministry colleague met me in the British Airway's lounge in Heathrow, and with one look at me said, "Duane, you gotta go home. You cannot make this trip."

His words were wise counsel and solid advice, but I was wrestling with what I should do. I had never "quit" on a trip before. While discussing how to get me well enough to make the eleven-hour flight, I ducked into the restroom just in time before becoming violently sick again. If you've ever flown overseas while sick to your stomach, you feel my pain.

AREN'T YOU HUPERMAN?

As I headed to the restroom, a man in a business suit started shouting, "Aren't you Huperman? It's Huperman!" His words shocked me; it took me a minute to realize what he was saying. I turned and nodded my head and said, "Yes, how did you know?" He proceeded to tell me how he'd seen it on TV in a hotel in Brussels. United Christian Broadcasters (UCB) TV in Europe had aired a recording of my Huperman message I preached at a large Christian conference in the UK.

The businessman went on to explain how the message of HUPER had changed his life for the better. To be honest, I was thinking, *If I don't make it to the restroom in the lounge ASAP, I'm about to change your day for the worse!* But soon after, as I sat in that restroom, that man's encouragement gave me the faith to get on that plane. God sent him to me at just the right time. It was a burst of encouragement to strengthen me to board the plane. Somehow the stewards overlooked my green composure and I made it to my seat.

Upon landing, I rejoiced that I had endured the flight. I checked into our hotel and crashed for the night. The next day, an unknown man met us in the lobby to take us to an undisclosed location. I still felt ill and grew weaker and weaker throughout the day. I received a note from the front desk from my longtime friend David Briggs, who was meant to be the other speaker at the four-day pastors' conference.

The note revealed that his traveling companion had passed kidney stones in Taipei and they would not be joining us. At that moment, I realized that if I had turned back, there would have been no speakers for the conference. These men and women risked their lives to attend the meetings. If caught, jail and great persecution would certainly await them. I couldn't have said, "I'm sorry. I got a stomach bug and can't make it!"

The next morning in Saigon, we waited in the hotel foyer praying for strength for the journey. Shortly afterward, a man approached me and said, "Mr. White?" "Yes," I replied. "I will be your guide for the day."

After getting in the van, he reported how the religious police raided the conference the first day, so they had fled to a different location. The new location was a two-hour journey up the Saigon River on a hydrofoil. It slowly dawned on me that I was about to ride on a boat in 110-degree heat for two hours with an upset stomach. Waves and heat are not the best combination for nausea! We prayed a quick prayer for healing and traveling grace.

Thankfully, I managed to keep my stomach reasonably calm for the duration of the boat ride. After we arrived, they immediately took us to the venue. I asked about the schedule, and they said, "You preach right now." "Oh great. How long?" I said. They replied, "Oh this session is just three to four hours!"

> They replied, "Oh this session is just three to four hours!"

I could not imagine how I would have the strength to preach for hours in 100-plus degree heat and extreme humidity in a packed room with no A/C. I continued to pray for strength beyond my natural ability.

Naturally, I needed a long nap, a shower, and possibly a doctor, but supernaturally I needed the power of God to use me to bless these hungry people who had traveled long distances and risked great peril to attend. Most had served prison sentences for their faith. Many had been beaten and raped and had their possessions stolen. They were very acquainted with the *"pressing, perplexing, persecuting and pushing down"* that 2 Corinthians 4 speaks of that most Americans can't fathom. *I must rally supernatural strength and healing so God can bless these beautiful saints*, I thought.

Hour after hour, I preached, prayed, and poured out my heart with a Word from God for them. I was soaking wet with sweat. Someone packed ice into wash cloths from the hotel and put them on my neck to help with the heat. As they tried to cool me off, I just kept preaching. Every session, I got stronger and stronger, and the anointing got stronger and stronger as I preached for four straight hours. Their faith and hunger helped me press past the sickness into God's presence. After that day, the sickness left me completely and I felt 100 percent restored.

Jehovah Rapha

Do you remember when God introduces Himself as Jehovah Rapha, I Am the Lord Who Heals? (See Exod. 15: 25-26) Three days after the fanfare of the Red Sea, Moses led the people into the wilderness. The celebration wore off because they were thirsty. No 7-Elevens were in sight on the corner of the desert. In the Western world, we take water for granted. We don't realize that it's earth's greatest commodity until we're the ones who are thirsty or wondering if the water's safe to drink. Finally, Moses came to Marah, but to his great disappointment the water was BITTER. People grumbled, and God instructed Moses to throw a tree into the water and the waters became sweet.

Jehovah Rapha = "I am the God that heals."

This is the first mention of God revealing Himself as our healer. Rapha in Hebrew means "sew back together, repairer." What did he need to repair? From this, a powerful picture foreshadowing the cross of Christ emerges. Jesus's sacrifice on the tree would heal the greatest originator of sickness: sin! As sin entered the world, sickness followed.

HEALING KELSEY

One Valentine's Day, my wife surprised me with a positive pregnancy test. We were thrilled to start our family. Originally, I had a five-year plan before kids, but somehow Kris persuaded me that was way too long. We immediately started praying and speaking healing over her womb. My birth defect had come out of nowhere in our family history, but then my nephew, Matthew, was born with the identical cleft lip and cleft palate. Thankfully, things have progressed drastically since I was born, but still it was no walk in the park for Matthew and all the surgeries he needed. (He's a huper hero!) We thought Matthew's cleft lip and palate was a weird accident, but with the birth of our firstborn, Kelsey, we would discover that the condition was indeed genetic.

On October 28, 1992, our beautiful blue-eyed bundle was born. After eighteen hours of labor, a doctor delivered her by cesarean section. This Christian South African doctor held her up, gestured for me to come over, and pointed to his lip and then hers. I must have looked confused. Right then, he looked at me and said, "She has a little cleft in her lip."

In that moment, joy and fear overwhelmed me. I was stunned. I had stood in faith and confessed the Word. How did this happen? The love and joy of being a daddy filled me, but still my heart sank fearing my child would have to walk through the same pain I had—and a little girl at that. For a boy, enduring this physical difference was one thing, but my baby girl? The doctor brought her over so we could see her, and in that holy moment, she smiled at us. Grace filled our hearts, and we knew God would provide for Kelsey Grace. He would make her bitter water sweet.

A few minutes later, our doctor said something profound: "It looks like someone tried to give this baby a cleft lip and God said, 'No it stops right here.'" He put her finger on the middle of her lip where the cleft stopped. She only had a partial cleft lip and no cleft palate. At that moment I realized our prayers had prevailed. It could have been so much worse. BUT GOD. She had a unilateral partial cleft lip that went halfway up her lip, but she had her palate! To repair her condition, she would only need one surgery when she was three months old.

We were thankful to gain the services of my nephew's doctor, who was one of the best in the world. As we sat in his waiting room, people from all over the world came to see him. Miraculously, we had insurance and would only have to pay a $1,000 deductible. If someone told me that today, I would do backflips for that amount, but at that time it might as well have been a million dollars compared to our budget. We prayed and believed that somehow God would make a way for Kelsey's lip to be healed.

A few weeks before the payment's due date, I went to the mailbox and almost fainted when I opened an anonymous letter with a cashier's check for exactly $1,000. We hadn't told anyone our need, but our HUPER God knew! It was a sweet day! God saw that day of redemption on my worst days as a kid in the hospital. I just had to live and believe to see it.

THE HEART OF THE FATHER

When we discuss healing, we have to come back to our simple "Caveman Theology." Remember? *God good! Devil bad!* The consequence of the fall and sin was sickness, but the redemption of sin on the cross was healing. This is hard for some people to theologically agree with, but if the cross was the atonement for sin, then it's the remedy for sickness and disease. The cross paid for our healing physically, emotionally, and mentally. It is finished. The war has been won, but now the manifestation of that work is being worked out into our natural lives.

It can be hard to understand why things don't manifest the way we want them to, but before we can understand why people aren't always healed, we have to have the right understanding of the Father's heart to heal. It is who He is—Jehovah Rapha. I believe it is God's will to heal, but we know that God doesn't always get His will or way. It's His will for all men to be saved, but many have rejected him. It's not His will when babies are aborted, but His will allows people to choose their own will. Even still, healing is who He is.

But for you who fear my name, the Sun of Righteousness will rise with healing in his wings. And you will go free, leaping with joy like calves let out to pasture. (Mal. 4:2 NLT)

Surely he took up our pain and bore our suffering, yet we considered him punished by God, stricken by him, and afflicted. But he was pierced for our transgressions, he was crushed for our

iniquities; the punishment that brought us peace was on him, and
by his wounds we are healed. (Isa. 53:4–5 NIV)

We see the heart of the Father lived out by the works of Jesus as the Great Physician. He was sent to earth to show us who the Father is. Jesus said He only says what the Father says, and He healed people because His heart was moved with compassion. (See Matt. 14:14.) That's who the Father is displayed in the life of the son.

John 10:10 tells us that Jesus's mission was to give us life and life more abundantly, but the devil comes to steal, kill, and destroy. He even commanded us in Matthew 10:8 to heal the sick. Why would He command us to do something that wasn't His will? Jesus commanded us to pray "your kingdom come, your will be done, on earth as it is in heaven." Is there any sickness in the kingdom? Of course not! So, Jesus was indicating that we are meant to bring the realities of the kingdom into this realm—on earth as it is in heaven.

Now, if we can move forward with the perspective that God is good and through the cross He has GIVEN healing, then we can talk about how we can RECEIVE it and let his power work in us to manifest that promise.

Do You Want to Be Healed?

I have always loved the story of Jesus healing the lame man at the pool of Bethesda. Let's look at some principles that we can learn from it.

Some time later, Jesus went up to Jerusalem for one of the Jewish festivals.
Now there is in Jerusalem near the Sheep Gate a pool, which in Aramaic is
called Bethesda and which is surrounded by five covered colonnades. Here
a great number of disabled people used to lie—the blind, the lame, the

paralyzed. One who was there had been an invalid for thirty-eight years. When Jesus saw him lying there and learned that he had been in this condition for a long time, he asked him, "Do you want to get well?" "Sir," the invalid replied, "I have no one to help me into the pool when the water is stirred. While I am trying to get in, someone else goes down ahead of me." Then Jesus said to him, "Get up! Pick up your mat and walk." At once the man was cured; he picked up his mat and walked. The day on which this took place was a Sabbath. (John 5:1–9 NIV)

For thirty-eight years this man had lain by this pool with his fellow sufferers. Perhaps he wasn't prepared for the Savior's response that day. The lame man tried to play the "victim card" on Jesus, but the Lord saw his excuse and raised an important question: ***Do you really want to be healed?*** The audacity of Jesus to ask that question. Do you really want a new identity from the one you've had for the last four decades? Healing would mean change. So, it's as if He asked him, "Do you really want to change?"

Next, the man plays the "magic" card on Him, but Jesus doesn't entertain the superstitious and mystical limitations of "lottery" healing. This was the day of healing because the Healer Himself was here. No special time or formula. Healing was a person. Jehovah Rapha manifested in Jesus the son. He tells him, "Get up! Pick up your mat and walk." This true HUPER healing moment broke through many layers of limitations and barriers. Jesus even healed him on the Sabbath! Whoa, how's that for breaking a barrier?

Let's break down the word **MAT** to help us see how Jesus challenged him to receive healing.

M = Move into Truth (GET UP!)

Jesus told the man to get up or rise up. In Greek, it is the powerful word *"egeirō,"* which means to awaken and rouse from sleep, from sitting or lying, from disease, from death. It's like someone is in a stupor and something startles them back to cognizance. That may be a simple one-word command, but huge implications were behind it!

Romans 10:17 tells us that faith comes by hearing and hearing the Word of God. *Faith begins where the will of God is known.* The lame man HEARD the word by Jesus, "Get up!" and he began to rise with the revelation of Jesus's word. How do I get faith? We don't "get" faith—faith comes. How? By hearing the Word of God and then revelation makes us rise.

> *So then faith comes by hearing, and hearing by the word of God.*
> (Rom. 10:17)

As we hear the Word, we start rising above the facts into God's truth, but we first need a revelation! How can we fight our feelings, our bitterness, and fears if we don't know there's a Savior?

> *Who Himself bore our sins in His own body on the tree, that we,*
> *having died to sins, might live for righteousness—by whose stripes*
> *you were healed.* (1 Pet. 2:24)

Okay, get this. It's good! Reread Isaiah 53:5 speaking prophetically *before* the cross (pre-cross). It says, *"By his wounds we are healed."* In between Isaiah and 1 Peter is the gospel—the cross which paid the penalty of all sins allowing us to walk in salvation and healing. Then Peter speaking *after* the cross (post-cross) quotes Isaiah 53, but this time it's changed to *were healed.*

Ephesians 2:8 tells us, "For by grace you have been saved through faith; and that not of yourselves, it is the gift of God." The word "saved" is the Greek word *"sozo,"* which means delivered from the penalties of judgment! The penalty of sin was sickness and by the cross, you have been delivered from the penalty! Our sin was placed on Jesus at the cross—our sickness, our mental anguish and anxiety, our fears, our hurts. But if we don't know this, how can we rise up in faith?

This revelation of truth will change the way you see healing. Think of how sanctification is to salvation as manifestation is to healing.

SALVATION> Leads to Sanctification (Received by Faith, Given by His Grace!)
HEALING > Leads to Manifestation (Received by Faith, Given by His Grace!)

Salvation deals with your UNSEEN (eternal) POSITION, while sanctification deals with your SEEN (temporary) CONDITION. HEALING is your UNSEEN POSITION, while manifestation of that healing deals with your SEEN CONDITION. Think about this. Two people receive Jesus as their Savior and give their life to Him. Both suffer from an addiction. The first person is instantly set free and never struggles with addiction again. The second person still struggles. It takes time and accountability to renew their mind and see them become freer. *Which one was more saved?*

Both were saved through faith by God's gift of grace. Each received the same gift. One had to walk out their salvation differently. It's kind of like when a chicken is hatching out of an egg. You can't help them or you can hurt them. Some people need the fight of faith for spiritual formation. It's a mystery. We don't know why.

It's the same with healing, received by faith given by grace. The price has been paid on the cross. *"By his wounds, we have been healed."* It is a mystery to us why it is manifested differently in people, but that doesn't mean they aren't healed! Some manifestations take more time or have different spiritual issues or circumstances we don't understand.

Here is a MAJOR truth bomb: Never let your SEEN CONDITION in this world dictate to you what you believe about your UNSEEN POSITION in Christ!

> *There are all kinds of FACTS and dysfunction, but the TRUTH is Jesus gave us a mandate for miracles."*

There are all kinds of FACTS and dysfunction, but the TRUTH is Jesus gave us a mandate for miracles. He wouldn't command us to do something that He didn't provide the power for. How could we do *"greater things than He did"* (John 14:12) if his power wasn't still available by grace.

Heal the sick, cleanse the lepers, raise the dead, cast out demons. Freely you have received, freely give. (Matt. 10:8)

A = Act in Faith

Next, Jesus told him to take up his MAT. Why did He say that? What did his mat represent? His paralysis was not only a physical condition, but after thirty-eight years it had become a culture—an identity. It represented his friends, his career, and his neighborhood. It actually might take MORE faith to pick up his mat because doing so would mean a change in mentality. Healing would mean a lot of changes for him. A change in friends. Who would he talk to? What would he talk about? Who would feel sorry for him? Did he really want to receive healing from being an "invalid" to "valid" because that validity would imply a lot of responsibility!

His mat labeled him with a mentality that lame was all he could ever be. It confined and limited him and those around him on their mats who would commensurate with him.

What's your mat? What excuses keep you pinned down to camp in the comfort of your mat? Labels like diabetic, cancer, or bipolar can limit us. These are all FACTS, but your diagnosis is not your destiny! These labels are not your identity! Stop identifying with the mat and answering to it by saying things like "my cancer," "my depression," "my bad back." You may have issues, but they are not WHO you are. Are you okay with that? Would you know who you are without your mat?

Initially this man had no faith. But, here Jesus challenges him. It would take faith to move his mat! Faith is seeing the unseen. Can you take up your mat by faith?

T = Trust the Lord

Get up. Pick up your mat and WALK! This word walk is *"peripateō,"* in the Greek which means "to make one's way, progress; to make due use of opportunities; follow; be occupied with." As we receive healing we act in faith and then walk it out. This is where we require TRUST with God's timing and way. It's funny that Jesus sees this same man later in the temple and encourages him to keep walking out his healing and not return to his old mat or it would be worse than before.

A short time later, Jesus found the man at the temple and said to him, "Look at you now! You're healed! Walk away from your sin so that nothing worse will happen to you. (John 5:14 TPT)

Sometimes Jesus healed people instantly by speaking over them. One time He rubbed mud in a blind man's eye. Another time He prayed multiple times for a man to see clearly. Yet another time a woman just touched Him and healing flowed from Him from her faith, and in another instance, only a few were healed because His hometown buddies were too familiar. Are you getting the point? There is no formula to follow. Healing is a person. Jehovah Rapha our Father, Jesus our Great Physician.

It's not your responsibility to manifest the miracle. It's our part to believe and know the HEALER. If we keep walking in the direction of healing, one day it will manifest itself even if we run out of time and step into heaven! Let's break this down.

PULLED INTO THE PROMISE

Reviewing from Chapter 5 on embracing the truth over the facts, remember our two realms: the SEEN and the UNSEEN. The SEEN are the facts of our disease, our symptoms, our diagnoses, our degenerative condition, our DNA, etc. The UNSEEN realm holds kingdom realities GRACE has provided that are waiting to be manifested. Truth exists UNMANIFESTED. Faith reaches into the UNSEEN and pulls the promise into the SEEN. As Jesus told us to pray, *"Your kingdom come . . . on earth as it is in heaven"* (Matt. 6:10). Faith can only apprehend what GRACE has already provided. Grace is God's responsibility, and faith is our responsibility—if you break down that word, it's our "ability to respond." But, God says He is the *author* and *finisher* of our faith! So it really all begins and ends with Him!

Faith deals with the UNSEEN. *The Amplified* version of Hebrews 11:1 says, "Now faith is the assurance (title deed, confirmation) of things hoped for (divinely guaranteed). . . ." What is a title deed? It's a legal document proving ownership. What if you suddenly discovered that a long-lost uncle left you an inheritance of oil-producing land worth millions? Your financial status just legally changed, but your bank account might still be empty! The title deed is the legal proof of a promised future possession.

What if your land is in hostile territory in the Middle East with terrorists claiming it as theirs? You legally own the land; you have the title, but you haven't possessed the promise yet. You've got to fight for it. *That is the fight of faith.* The battle is to possess or mani-fest the promise of God not positionally, but experientially. It's ours legally, in Christ, but must be received vitally.

We've studied how, like Abraham, faith is credited to our account when we believe, not when we receive the full manifesta-tion, so what is the variable? TIME. The by-product (manifestation) of my faith is not the evidence I have faith. Belief followed by an appropriate corresponding action is that proof. If in faith we run out of TIME in this natural life, then the UNSEEN pulls us into the promise! Hebrews exhibits it's "hall of fame" in Chapter 11, where we see in verse 13 that there are those who died IN FAITH not receiving their promise.

These all died in faith, not having received the promises, but having seen
them afar off were assured of them, embraced them and confessed that they
were strangers and pilgrims on the earth. (Heb. 11:13)

This is where the "faith message" veered off at times, judging or shaming people for having weak faith or no faith if they didn't receive their healing or miracle breakthrough. Would you be so bold to look at the martyrs of the New Testament and tell them they didn't have faith because they weren't miraculously delivered? If we run out of time, we run into eternity!

 *If we run out of time, we run into eternity!"*

I wish I had great explanations for why people don't always receive the manifestation of their healing immediately or even on earth. I love how Bill Johnson says, *"In order to have a peace that surpasses all understanding, you have to give up your right to understand."* I don't understand why my retina detached and I'm legally blind in my left eye, but I receive my healing and will keep walking it out. I don't understand why my faith-filled friends, Pastor Paul Godawa (Poland) and Rich Hubbard (UK), both powerful men of God, died without seeing their healing from cancer on earth, but I can tell you one thing—they both ran into the arms of Jesus, the Almighty Healer, and stepped into the full manifestation of their healing in heaven. They may have run out of time on earth, but they ran into their promise in eternity!

We live in the mysterious tension of the NOW and the NOT YET, and we trust Him in the gaps. You can sum it up like this: "What if = FEAR, Even if = FAITH."

HEALING CODY

When we got pregnant with our son, Cody, the sonographer said she saw a cleft lip and wanted to order an expensive sonogram to examine it. We had to wait a month before having the sonogram, and in that time, we asked everyone we knew with faith to pray over my wife's belly. We stood and believed that Cody was healed. We named him Cody Josiah. Josiah means "the Lord has healed, and the fire of God."

Finally, when the special sonogram was performed, doctors couldn't find any cleft. The sonogram technician couldn't believe it. She showed us both and said, "There is nothing there this time." He was born completely healed.

Now, get this—Kelsey was just as healed as Cody. Maybe Kelsey's manifestation was different. Maybe she has a greater capacity to receive grace and compassion for others who've faced that issue. Maybe her manifestation allows a greater grace for healing to flow through her. The other day Kelsey took her son, Zion, to the doctor's office for a cough. While in the waiting room, she noticed a mom holding an infant with a cleft lip. Kelsey shared with the mom how she'd had a cleft lip as well. The mom stared at Kelsey through tears and unloaded all the questions and fears she'd stored up. Kelsey administered a healing balm to that mom's heart that no one else could give unless received firsthand. Healed people heal other people.

We hear all the time how *hurt people hurt people.* Wouldn't it be amazing if the church was filled with *healed people who heal people?* That sounds pretty HUPER to me. Let's get up, take our mat, and walk out our healing in the presence of the Healer.

[9]

HUPER PROVISION: HEAVEN'S FLOW OF KINGDOM
FINANCE

> *But since you excel in everything—in faith, in speech, in*
> *knowledge, in complete earnestness and in the love we have*
> *kindled in you—see that you also excel in this grace of*
> *giving."*
> —2 Cor. 8:7 NIV

OUR YOUNG FEMALE friend walked in a Houston mall with her
disobliging mother when a jewelry shop caught her eye. She spotted
a diamond tennis bracelet and remarked how pretty it was. "If you
keep giving your life to serve Jesus, you can forget about ever
having anything that nice!" her mom quipped. Our friend kept
walking with a peace in her pocket that she could never out give
God whether her return was diamonds or heavenly treasure. He
was worth it.

My childhood was filled with the dichotomy of my dad, the
dreamer, believing his "big break" was always around the next
corner versus the reality of my mom trying to keep us afloat. Most
years we struggled to have Christmas presents, not to mention
paying the bills. My mom was assigned the task of telling my sister

and me how "we simply can't afford that." The narrative in my head became "You better fight for everything you have or you'll never have anything." Sound familiar? Jesus said He wouldn't leave us as orphans, but many of us live with an orphan mentality and fear never having enough. As the saying goes, "You better get all you can, can all you get, and then sit on the can!"

As a teenager working to help my mom make the house payment, that fear of "not enough" or fight of "don't take it from me" majorly limited my life. Whether it's a fear of lack or the fight to avoid lack, the struggle and the insecurity driving it is the same and originates from the devil's first lie: "You better provide for yourself, because God is holding out on you."

> *"The thief does not come except to steal, and to kill, and to destroy. I have come that they may have life, and that they may have it more abundantly."* (John 10:10)

HOARDING OR HUPER

In the church we like to call it a "poverty spirit" or, lately, a "scarcity mentality." It resembles an orphan mentality—not trusting you have a provider who truly cares. A poverty or orphan mindset sees the cup as being half empty while a "sonship" mentality sees the cup as being REFILLABLE by your Father! (We talked about being a part of the family in Chapter 6.)

I have many friends who have adopted children out of poverty. It took time to transform their thinking from the fear of deprivation. The parents would find food hidden in their children's pockets and under pillows until the children began to trust them to provide daily, making hoarding unnecessary. We can never live as cheerful kingdom givers if we're afraid God won't really provide. There is a grace to transform us from HOARDING graspers, limited to our ability and means, to HUPER givers, unlimited by the Father's supply!

Of course poverty is relative. I'm not proposing a pie in the sky, claim your pink Cadillac gospel, but I *can* testify to the power of how God transformed my FEAR into FAVOR. Whether I was rejoicing as a teenager because I miraculously made it to my destination running on fumes with no money to refill my gas tank (true story) or if I had plenty to fill up someone else's tank, it's a mindset of position and identity, not an amount in the bank, that dictates our joy.

Once while preaching in Africa, I asked a group of leaders to pray and ask God to define prosperity for them. One of my African friends described prosperity as having salt on his table for every meal. A year later, he was praising God because He had provided salt every day that year! Prosperity is relative. Sonship is a relationship with a God who provides. He actually introduces Himself to us as "Jehovah Jireh, the God who will provide." A name means a nature, and God provided a ram for Abraham to sacrifice on Mount Moriah. This symbolized how God would provide for us a Savior who would be our ultimate provision.

With my meager upbringing, you would never pick me as one God would use to break others out of poverty thinking and into HUPER generosity, but amazingly, that's what He's done! Only God! My transformation started as I received the revelation that my life is not limited to me but by God's power BEYOND ME! I have an inheritance IN CHRIST beyond my family name, wealth or reputation.

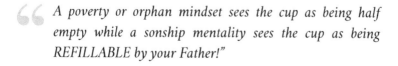

A poverty or orphan mindset sees the cup as being half empty while a sonship mentality sees the cup as being REFILLABLE by your Father!"

This revelation causes radical shifts in behavior. Instead of hoarding selfishly, you're challenged to sow joyfully! Kris and I determined when we married that we would live a generous life beyond ourselves. God had radically transformed both of us from poverty thinking, and we made a covenant together that we would always endeavor to pray and hear God in our giving and trust him to provide for our living.

Kris learned many lessons in trusting God for finances as a child. God taught her at a young age to obey when He said to sow and then be ready to receive when He blessed her back. At age sixteen, all her other friends were getting cars, but her family could not afford the same for her. Still God challenged Kris to believe Him for a car because He was her provider!

> God can get it TO US if he knows he can get it THROUGH US."

Kris's mom had a favorite gold chain with an anchor charm. The chain broke, and she didn't know when she'd be able to replace it. God told Kris to give her mom her own gold chain and sow it believing God would provide a car in His timing. She obeyed, blessed her mom, and out of the blue God blessed her with a car. Now, she had to believe God for it to start every morning, but hey, she rejoiced for small beginnings and was so thankful for that first car. Kris and I have now had the privilege of giving away several cars!

RESERVOIRS OF KINGDOM RESOURCE

Our friends Mike and Chandra Noviskie are doing great work in South Africa in one of the poorest townships running a preschool project called Berakah. With around 47 percent of the population unemployed and the other half making very little money, poverty is a challenge for this marginalized people group. I love how Chandra expresses her heart in training her teachers to think differently. She tells them, "Even though you live in poverty, poverty doesn't have to live in you!"

A few years into our marriage, God spoke to my sister, Donna, to give Kris her diamond tennis bracelet. It was the nicest thing Kris had ever owned. It meant the world to her that God would use her sister-in-law to bless her in such an exceptional way. She only wore it on special occasions, and one of those special days happened to be when our friends Jamie and Lea Peters were ministering at our church.

Kris said that as she raised her hand in worship and glanced at the bracelet on her arm, she knew it was no longer hers. She was called to bless Lea with it. In the kingdom of God, "stuff or resources" flow *to us* and then *through us* when God directs. God can get it TO US if he knows he can get it THROUGH US. Kris blessed Lea with the bracelet knowing that she might not have another bracelet like that for some time but that her kingdom investment in Africa was a greater blessing than any carbon formation could ever be.

 Even though you live in poverty, poverty doesn't have to live in you!"

- CHANDRA NOVISKIE

Sometime later, Kris traveled to Burundi with me to see the Peters. Their church leadership team greeted us and gave everyone gifts—except Kris. She was actually relieved because it's so humbling and hard to receive gifts from them. Before we left that day, Mama Jackie said, "We waited until the end to give Kris a gift.

This is the most precious thing I own. You have sent your husband here so many times during the war and now you have come to be with us as well, and I want to bless you with this."

Mama Jackie and her husband were national pastors serving with Jamie and Lea. With a big smile, she handed Kris a diamond tennis bracelet! She had received the bracelet as a gift from Lea, not knowing that it had originated from Kris! That seed came full circle after a few years. When we obey God and give, it forges a reservoir for future blessings to be strategically supplied at the proper time for His Kingdom purpose! Don't block your future blessings. Keep the flow going! We are blessed to be a blessing.

GRACE TO GIVE

Are you ready for our HUPER giving Scripture? You knew it was coming, right? In 2 Corinthians 8, the apostle Paul teaches us about the grace to give beyond ourselves! He encourages the church in Corinth to follow the example of the believers in Macedonia.

> *Moreover, brethren, we make known to you the grace of God*
> *bestowed on the churches of Macedonia: that in a great trial of*
> *affliction the abundance of their joy and their deep poverty*
> *abounded in the riches of their liberality. For I bear witness that*
> *according to their ability, yes, and beyond their ability, they were*
> *freely willing.* (2 Cor. 8:1–3)

Paul challenges the wealthier Corinthian Christians with the story of how the Macedonians, even in their impoverished situations, wanted to spread the gospel and give to their ability and BEYOND their ability. That Greek word for beyond is, you guessed it—*HUPER*! How can you give beyond your ability? You can only do what you can do, right? You can't squeeze blood out of a turnip, as they say. BUT, when God gets involved with your seed, His power takes what you can do and blesses it BEYOND in huper ways! That's called supernatural increase!

Paul tells them how they have excelled in every area, but then he implores them to excel in this grace also. What grace is that? The grace to give!

But as you abound in everything—in faith, in speech, in knowledge, in all diligence, and in your love for us—see that you abound in this grace also.
(2 Cor. 8:7)

The Corinthian church was NOT poor like the Macedonian church. Corinth was the place to be if you had a fat wallet. There is a famous ancient saying that goes, *"Ou pantos plein es Korinthon,"* which translates as "not everyone is able to go to Corinth" (due to the expensive living standards that prevailed in the city). But interestingly, Paul doesn't condemn the Corinthians for having money. He just encourages them to give beyond themselves! Wealth does not threaten God. Under the old covenant, He offered it as a promise.

And you shall remember the Lord your God, for it is He who gives you power to get (create) wealth, that He may establish His covenant which He swore to your fathers, as it is this day. (Deut. 8:18)

God promised Abraham prosperity if he followed and obeyed Him, and all through the Old Testament part of God's covenant with His kids was prosperity.

"And God is able to make all grace abound toward you, that you, always having all sufficiency in all things, may have an abundance for every good work." (2 Cor. 9:8)

There are so many misconceptions and extremes around money. One extreme thought: Jesus was "poor" and you should be too. The other extreme thought: Every believer is called to be a millionaire, and if you follow a faith formula you'll be prosperous. The truth is found in the balance. God is always concerned with our hearts. You could be a pauper on the street who gave all his worldly possessions to the poor and be prouder than the CEO in his Lexus who's using his wealth to fund microfinance projects around the world. We cannot judge from the outside appearance. Haven't we learned anything?

Jesus taught us with the Pharisees—it's about the heart, not religious acts or bank account amounts. Do you have a KINGDOM heart? Do you have a grace to give beyond you? As my friend Mark Hankins always says, "God doesn't mind you have Mercedes living if you have Mercedes giving!" Or, we could say, God will bless you with HUPER living if you have HUPER giving!

Now, Paul continues his thoughts to the church in Corinth all the way through chapters 8 and 9. Boy, he's serious about getting this idea across!

Now may He who supplies seed to the sower, and bread for food, supply and multiply the seed you have sown and increase the fruits of your righteousness. (2 Cor. 9:10)

This verse introduces the idea that God will give us seed and bread! Seed is our investment for the future, and bread meets our need for today. Matthew 6 tells us how He knows what the birds need—don't we trust that He cares about what we need? He knows, and He cares! Seeds can come in many forms besides money or our treasure. Seeds can also be time, talent, and influence. The problem is that many of us eat our seed and sow our bread! What?

This is an issue of stewardship, discipline, and hearing God direct us. Many times God gives you a job to provide bread, so don't give it away by not appreciating it and getting fired. But, on the other hand, when He blesses you, ask Him, "Lord, is this seed or bread?" I'm a firm believer in tithing and over-and-above giving because it always leaves a boundary to allow seed and bread to flow in your life. If you're a person who believes tithing is under the law (tithing preceded the law with Melchizedek) and want to live in New Testament grace, then let the apostle Paul challenge you to give *beyond your ability* like the Macedonians.

If the Old Testament was the firstfruits or 10 percent, then the New Covenant should be way beyond the law. Grace much more abounds! So you should be excited about giving much more than 10 percent by the New Testament grace that supersedes the law!

Give, and it will be given to you. A good measure, pressed down, shaken together and running over, will be poured into your lap. For with the measure you use, it will be measured to you. (Luke 6:38 NIV)

He Can Afford It

Before we planted our church, The Bridge in Denton, Texas, in 2007, I drove around the city looking for a house. I prayed, "God, I really hate looking for houses and wasting time. Can You just show me where it is?" I was driving down a road I had never been on and saw a handwritten "For Sale by Owner" sign. I turned and pulled up to a beautiful English manor house that I knew my wife would love! I got the flyer for it and went home and showed it to my family at dinner. "I think God showed me our house!" I proclaimed as I laid down the flyer. The kids readily agreed, "We love it!"

Kris looked up at me and literally laughed out loud. She said, "Duane, do you know how much this house will cost? They didn't put the price on the flyer for a reason! This is way beyond us!" I said, "Yes, it's definitely HUPER, and when God gives it to us it will be beyond us and for his glory!" Kris now admits how she repented because she felt like Sarah laughing at God's promise. Long story, God did give us that house. It was a miracle, and we started our church there in the living room.

That's a HUPER testimony, but I also want to tell you what happened years later. God told us to sell the English manor house, and we ultimately built a house in a beautiful little country town called Argyle. We enjoyed it and lived there for about two years; then God gave us our church building in the north of the city. We had a thirty-minute drive to the church and knew we needed to be closer. We obeyed and sacrificed our new home to be closer to the church. We bought a simple fixer-upper, and for a while it would have seemed like a major setback.

We worked to improve the house for resale. Then, the time came and God gave us a new house five minutes from the church, which was even greater than the one we'd built. Why do I share this? It's all wood and mortar—it's all earth. Houses come and go, cars come and go, money comes and goes—it's a flow! If we learn how to trust God and not hold on when He says sow—how to be content when He says stay—He truly works all things together for good and not only blesses us but creates a flow of blessings!

Who Is Your Source?

Many times, we're guilty of telling our kids, "We would do that, but we don't have the money." What made the decision? Money. What is directing your destiny? Money. Who then is your God? God convicted me years ago to change my language and decision making with my kids. They wanted a bike. *Okay, we are choosing not to spend our money on that right now because we need to give you food and a house, but you can pray and ask God if He wants you to have it—He's your source, not us.* I trained my kids to think this way, but sometimes God laughs when they come back to remind me of it!

My youngest daughter, Ashton, has loved Africa since she was around three years old. She was playing near the TV when a program about feeding kids in Kenya came on. She put down her toys and boldly said, "I do that!" Since then, that's all she's dreamed about. On career day in the fourth grade, she dressed in her African outfit with a baby tied to her back. Her teacher questioned what profession she represented, and Ashton replied, "An orphanage runner, of course!"

After much prayer and counsel, Ashton chose to study nursing and gain a skill to serve the people and open doors for the gospel. She earned a scholarship to our local university, which is a renowned nursing school. This was a great plan! She could stay home and have university completely paid for. *NICE!* It *was* nice, but it wasn't HUPER. Ashton dreamed of attending Oral Roberts University and believed God put it in her heart even though it would be a huge stretch and require a lot more money!

Oral's vision to "raise up students to hear My voice, to go where My light is dim, where My voice is heard small, and My healing power is not known, even to the uttermost bounds of the earth," resounded in her spirit. Ashton said, "Dad, I know you're not my source. I don't expect you to pay for it, but I'm believing if God wants me to go, then He will make a way for me!" She received scholarships but still needed large sums each semester to stay in school.

Every semester stretched her faith, but God made a way, many times down to the wire! Funny story. One day I got a call from my friend Joe Glass, who now cheers us on from heaven. He said that strangely the card on their refrigerator with Ashton's picture on it fell off and landed on his feet. God instructed him to tell Ashton's *earthly* father that her *heavenly* Father was going to provide for her. He said, "I know you know that, but I felt impressed to call and tell you." BOOM! That call helped me pass through the financial SEEN barrier into God's UNSEEN provision that was beyond my plan.

In Ashton's junior year, she received a surprise gift from Joe's widow, Brenda Glass. As she held the envelope, the Holy Spirit whispered to her, "This is a seed. Sow it." Thinking it might be a couple of hundred dollars, she nearly fell over when she saw that it was $5,000. God marked it for SEED even though it could have met part of her immediate need. She gave beyond her ability and beyond what made sense to her mind but made perfect sense to her spirit! We hear the catchy phrase, *"If it's not enough to meet your need, it's not your harvest. It must be your seed."* But the key is listening to the Spirit who earmarks the difference. She gave the money to a missionary couple going to Cape Town to serve in a football outreach. It was their BREAD, the exact amount they needed to finish their support.

Ashton's vision was much bigger than one semester of tuition, and a seed planted into missions was a great investment in her future—and God miraculously provided for her tuition too. Every year at ORU was a lesson in faith for her, but God made a way. He wasn't ever early, but every semester He was right on time! She graduated in 2019 and had HUPER favor to receive a residency at Children's Medical Center in Dallas working in the pediatric ICU.

Ashton's big faith wasn't built in that moment at college. Just like for my wife and I, it began when she was young and in mundane, seemingly insignificant ways. She saw many miraculous meetings where I ministered and the Spirit would whisper to her to give things. One day, when she was about four, I was preaching at a church and she walked up and put her favorite shoes on the stage. She told me, "Daddy, God wants me to give my shoes." I answered, "Okay, Ashton, but you're going to have to walk to the car and lunch barefoot!" After the service, the usher tried to return her shoes. She was highly offended. She said, "Daddy, this man won't take my offering!" With a grin, I told him he had better take it. That day it might have seemed silly to the usher, but it was serious to God because He was molding Ashton to hear Him.

You thought Kris's bracelet story was over, didn't you? We started with the story of our friend in Houston looking at the diamond bracelet in the shop window and her mom saying she'd never have anything like that if she served Jesus. A few days later, Kris and I went to speak at this friend's church. God told Kris, who knew nothing of the story, to give her bracelet to this friend. Tears flowed down the woman's cheeks. It wasn't about a piece of jewelry. It was about God's lavish love for her and confirmation of her choice to serve Him.

You should have seen her mom's face when she saw the bracelet! Huper giving is really fun! We don't know where the bracelet went from there, but my wife has received more jewelry that she's sown all over the world. She's lost count because it's a lifestyle—not a loss. It's a flow!

PROVISION IN POLAND

I have witnessed many supernatural HUPER financial miracles, but I'll end with this story. One of my best friends and partners in ministry was a Polish pastor named Paul Godawa. We met him and his wife, Joanna, at a special gathering of ministers, hosted by Tony and Kathy Miller, in the mountains of Tennessee. God radically saved Paul and called him to start a Christian church in Koszalin, Poland. Most churches there are Orthodox Catholic, so this calling required great courage and also came at a great cost.

Paul and Joanna planted the church in Koszalin and needed a building. One day a random businessman who wasn't from Koszalin met with Paul and handed him a bag filled with money. The mystery man said it was for the building Paul was believing for. After he left, he opened the bag to find $100,000, which was enough to buy the building, move into it, and begin to renovate it into a church home.

Their church grew with favor across the nation and Pastor Paul produced thousands of cassette tapes and CDs with the gospel, pioneering faith across Poland. One year, Paul invited me to do the final session at his conference because most of the other speakers had returned home. He asked for a coffee meeting beforehand to share his vision. He shared how they believed God wanted to give them upgraded cameras to film his television program that would air on all public Polish television stations. They had a strategic opportunity to access homes around the nation.

I said, "Great. How much do you need?" He answered, "Eighty-eight thousand dollars." I tried not to blink. "American money? How much do you have now?" He replied, "About $10,000." *Man, praise the Lord.* He continued, "That's why you're here." I said, "Well, I'd love to give you that much, but that's not in my bank account." He said, "I don't need your money. I need your faith." *Okay, I can give that!*

I went back to the hotel room and told Kris, "Well, this is going to be God. We'll trust Him and see what He does."

That night I shared a message close to my heart called "Consumers and Producers." After I shared, a spirit of faith and generosity moved in the place in a supernatural way. People began to bring things and lay them on the stage to sow for the television camera purchase. One pastor gave a sound system he had sitting in storage, another brought his keys and gave his car! People brought cash, coats, jewelry, watches, and televisions. If they didn't have it with them, they wrote down what they desired to give.

These were not wealthy people. At the time the average monthly income was about $400 to $500. It was BEYOND them. It was a HUPER move of God! After everything was counted, the total offering was over $80,000! That one offering purchased cameras that broadcast the gospel throughout Poland on public television when few others were doing so. Only heaven will tell of the impact of the message reaching into homes and saving hearts. But BEYOND that amazing joy, that night God broke people free from poverty mentalities and released a HUPER spirit of faith and grace to give.

 Money spent is temporary; money sown is eternal.

Huper Giving Is Eternal

Paul alludes to this in this challenge to the Corinthians. Our gifts sown in faith are eternal. *"As it is written: He has dispersed abroad, He has given to the poor; His righteousness endures forever"* (2 Cor. 9:9). We see this thought repeated in Acts 10 when Cornelius the Gentile is described as a devout man.

"And when he observed him, he was afraid, and said, "What is it, lord?" So he said to him, "Your prayers and your alms have come up for a memorial before God." (Acts. 10:4)

This blows my mind! Every offering I have ever given is still in heaven before the Lord. Money that I *spend* leaves my life forever, but money I *sow* into the kingdom is forever in my heavenly future before the Lord! Money spent is temporary; money sown is eternal. Giving is one of our biggest joys and greatest graces. It launches us into a life WAY BEYOND what we could ever provide for ourselves whether we reap it with blessings on earth or true treasures in heaven. Let us be heaven hoarders and HUPER givers—BEYOND us!

Don't keep hoarding for yourselves earthly treasures that can be stolen by thieves. Material wealth eventually rusts, decays, and loses its value. Instead, stockpile heavenly treasures for yourselves that cannot be stolen and will never rust, decay, or lose their value. For your heart will always pursue what you value as your treasure. (Matt. 6:19–21 TPT)

10

BREAKTHROUGH POWER: LAUNCHING THE BRIDGE

> *Big ideas come from forward-thinking people who challenge the norm, think outside the box, and invent the world they see inside rather than submitting to the limitations of current dilemmas."* —T. D. Jakes

EVERY SUPERHERO NEEDS SUPERPOWERS, and every *huper* hero needs *huper* powers! *"Now unto him that is able to do exceeding abundantly above all that we ask or think, ACCORDING TO THE POWER that worketh in us . . ."* (Eph. 3:20 KJV). It's wonderful to talk about destiny and potential, but unless we activate the power to change ourselves and break through the barriers limiting us, then it hides dormant.

ACCORDING TO THE POWER

God's power in my life is equal to the proportion I allow Him to work through me. God's heart is always relationship. He invites us to partner with Him. Remember 2 Corinthians 4:7? We yield our vessel to see His power work miraculously in us.

OUR YIELDED WEAKNESS + HIS HUPER POWER =
HUPER LIFE

The powerful phrase "according to" seems like an insignificant preposition, but it is a huge indicator pointing to the source of power. *Merriam-Webster's Dictionary* says it means "in conformity with, as stated or attested by, depending on." It is in direct relation to and in proportion with. Smith Wigglesworth said, *"In me is working a power stronger than every other power. The life that is in me is a thousand times bigger than I am outside."* If we saw our lives like this, maybe we would experience more miracles like Mr. Wigglesworth.

IT'S PAID FOR

Has anyone ever given you a gift card? That card has been prepaid for you to use, but in itself it's just a piece of plastic. Its ability is proportionate to the prepaid amount applied to the card. See where I'm going with this? The cross of Jesus Christ prepaid and filled your card with the power for you to utilize for your purpose in His kingdom! How many gift cards sit unused in wallets? It's not the giver's fault that they haven't been redeemed. They are in the possession of the recipient, but the resource hasn't been utilized because it's waiting on an ACT of faith by the recipient to use it! They can't "see" the resource on the card. They have to trust it's been credited to them.

I pray that you will continually experience the immeasurable greatness of God's power made available to you through faith. Then

*your lives will be an advertisement of this immense power as it
works through you!. . . (Eph. 1:19 TPT)*

The HUPER word in verse 19 for "immeasurable" (exceeding
in NKJV) is *huperballo*. Remember, it means "to surpass in throwing, to throw over or beyond anything; excel or be in a greater
degree." The next word is "greatness" (*megathos*), which means
"extreme in greatness or extent." God's HUPER greatness is in you
waiting to burst your opposition and barriers! But how? Through
faith—seeing the unseen! I believe God is stirring your faith even
now to throw you over your obstacles. That's called BREAK-
THROUGH!

Rain Up!

In the Old Testament, the anointing came "upon" men or women.
They received the anointing for tasks at hand. For example, the
anointing came upon Elijah, and he ran faster than the chariots of
Ahab to Jezreel. The Bible tells us that he girded up his loins—that
means he pulled up his trousers, and he ran! How did he do that? He
did it by the anointing that came upon him.

In the New Testament, the anointing comes "out of" us. We have
an anointing—an unction from the Holy One—and it is inside.
Instead of God's power raining down on us from a task, it rains up
and out of us! If you are a born-again Spirit-filled believer, stop
looking for your strength to come from someone or something else
—it's in you! The life of God is a gift residing in you—the treasure
in jars of clay. But it's there not just to look pretty but to break the
powers of darkness and advance God's kingdom on the earth.
Power is pointless unless it has a purpose!

You are of God, little children, and have overcome them, because He who is
in you is greater than he who is in the world. (1 John 4:4)

Let's shift our thinking from praying for God to move ON US to praying that the life of God IN US will flow OUT OF US! Paul instructed his protégé Timothy to stir up the gift of God that was in him. It had been imparted to him and needed to be stirred and released! (See 2 Tim. 1:6.) When we sing that great chorus, *"Let it rain, let it rain. Open the floodgates of heaven,"* we realize that heaven is IN US! So, when I open my mouth in praise, or to declare my faith, or to speak the Word over my situation, I am making it RAIN! I'm not waiting for it to RAIN DOWN on me, I am letting it RAIN UP through me! We HAVE this treasure IN jars of clay.

REDEEM THE TIME

God created you for a HUPER assignment, a purpose that requires His power. Every life, from every nation, from every era is linked to God's kingdom purpose for His grand plan. Every season of your life has strategic moments that can only be accessed in that perfect timing. The New Testament describes time in two terms: *chronos* and *kairos*.

Chronos: *duration, space of time, succession, general time* [1]
Kairos: *divine, strategic appointments, epoch making opportunity, window in time* [2]

Chronos is the duration, space of time, or succession of our life, such as in calendar time—day in and day out. *Kairos* is strategic time, or military time. It's a special term to describe divine, strategic appointments intersecting with *chronos* time—seasons God has layered into every stage of our lives. It's a window of opportunity, but it's a closing window. I call them "divine appointments" because they represent markers in time.

Every opportunity of a lifetime has to be seized in the lifetime of the opportunity! You cannot step in the same river twice. You say, "What? Yes, you can. You step in, step out, and step in again." No, wait. You can step in and out, but when you step back in again, the river is different! The river runs. It has changed. You can never step in the same river twice because it's moved. We must seize those God-appointed moments because they will never come around the same way again! If we are faithful in the *chronos*, God will provide the kairos!

> **Redeem:** (Greek = *exagarazo*) *to buy up for your own use; to buy up ALL that is available to be used* [3]

In Ephesians 5:16, we are encouraged to *"make the most of every opportunity"* (NIV), or as the *King James Version* reads, *"redeem the time,"* and the word for time is *kairos*.

Be very careful, then, how you live—not as unwise but as wise, making the most of every opportunity, because the days are evil. (Eph. 5: 15-16 NIV)

What does it mean to "redeem time"? Redeem is the Greek word *exagarazo*, which means "to buy up for your own use; to buy up ALL that is available to be used." How do you buy time?

You can't use dollars, pounds, or yen. Thayer's and Strong's both say, "You buy time not with currency but with zeal and passionate obedience." That sounds to me like someone acting in faith to release the power that's been prepaid for them! But with this opportunity evil comes to oppose it.

. . .

OPPORTUNITY AND OPPOSITION

Growing up I heard this Scripture with the word evil dramatically stressed over the word opportunity. You can imagine it quoted with a great King James scary preacher voice. *"Redeem the time for the days are EVVVVVVVIL!"* This evokes more fear for what the devil can do than God. Different words are used for evil in the New Testament. *Kakós* is evil in the general overall wicked sense, but the word used here in Ephesians 5 is *ponēros*, where we get our word *pernicious*. This is an evil with a direct assignment against the good or the *kairos* moment God has for you to redeem!

Strong's describes it as "toils, pressures and annoyances." Have you ever launched out of your comfort zone with a dream from God and then hit a hard wall of opposition? It's tempting to cry, "Why me, God?" But in the light of this Scripture, it makes perfect sense. If you weren't a threat, there would be no ploy to stop you. Of course the devil's going to oppose it!

Job said, *"You shall laugh at destruction and famine . . ."* (Job 5:22). Trouble is not funny, so why did he say that? Maybe the devil's opposition has been painful in your life. People disappoint us, life distracts us, things annoy us. But compared to God's exceedingly great HUPER power, the devil's attempts are laughable if we see them in the light of eternity.

Remember 2 Corinthians 4:17? These light momentary afflictions are producing in me a weight of glory! What is your pain producing? The pain is not greater than the purpose. The pain is not greater than the HUPER power, unless we let it be. The devil wants the pain to become a prison keeping us from breaking through the barrier and talk us out of our divine assignment. He's provided breakthrough power to help us PUSH THROUGH the opposition! With every door of opportunity there is an opposition to block it. Although the opposition is great, we are more than overcomers!

. . .

The Bridge to Beyond

Kris and I knew that God put church planting in our hearts. I've told you how if you cut me I bleed missions and local church! We were enjoying growing Beyond These Shores, and I was traveling over 200,000 air miles a year. It didn't make sense in the natural to shift energy toward a local body, but Kris and I could sense God's *kairos* moment coming. We moved back from serving in England to base ourselves in Decatur, Texas.

It was very humbling and redeeming moving back to my home-town and facing the ghosts of the past with the power of the present. But, whenever we drove through Denton (the "big city" about thirty minutes away from Decatur) with our family, an excite-ment would stir in all of us. I describe it by saying "it made my baby leap"—just as Elizabeth's baby leapt within her when she saw Mary.

Kris and I were pregnant with a dream: a church that would reach, as Dale Gentry prophesied, "all ages, all races, and all kinds." We love Denton because it is a melting pot of cultures. The univer-sities draw people from around the world, and Denton has a distinct expression of being diverse and unique. If God was calling us back to the United States, at least it was to a city that has cultures that represent the world.

One day as we shopped in the Denton mall, a group of teenage boys caught my eye. They looked like they might be up to no good, lingering around and aimlessly loitering. At this mall I experienced a *kairos* moment. As I pondered how we are faced with a fatherless generation and how these young men desperately needed to know the love of "a father," I heard the Spirit of God say to my heart, "You're right—they don't have a father. Will you do it?" The river was running. Would I jump in or stay on the shore?

I knew this was God's confirmation to plant in Denton and raise up a multiethnic community of believers to bridge God's life to a fatherless generation. I felt like Paul when he said in 1 Corinthians 16:9, *"A great and effective door has opened to me, and there are many adversaries."* God had invited us into a great adventure, but many adversaries were out there.

"A huge door of opportunity for good work has opened up here. (There is also mushrooming opposition.)" (1 Cor. 16:9 MSG)

Thanks to our generous Beyond These Shores partners, we miraculously raised the money to launch what would become The Bridge Church. I strongly felt God urge me to say we were "launching," not planting, the church. God called an amazing launch team to assist us with the mission. Some even relocated from Florida, Georgia, and the UK! Actually, few people on the team were from Denton. It was a wonderfully diverse team. It's easy to look back now with nostalgia and think how wonderful those days were— now that we're on the other side of the opposition, that is.

Excitement and passion filled us to "connect people to life" in Denton. We prayed, worshipped, and planned outreaches in the living room of our new Denton house. God helped us with creative ideas to reach people in a nonreligious way. We paid for a billboard over a Hooters restaurant with the name of our website, findthebridge.com, and the question, "Have you found the bridge?" We sent flyers out with the same question, and people wore T-shirts around town for us, so the question seemed to appear everywhere you looked.

At first, we thought we would launch in September, but in our prayer meetings the team agreed that the divine date was Easter 2007. We would have diaper drives, mow lawns, hold Easter egg hunts in multiple places around the city, and give away prizes like bikes and gaming stations. Then we would invite people to church the next day to have the chance to win a grand prize for our grand opening!

Our friend Tyrone Lister introduced us to an amazing woman named Charlye Heggins, the first African-American councilwoman in Denton. She represented one of the districts that burned in our hearts to reach. When Jesus sent the disciples into the city, He told them to find the "man of peace." Councilwoman Heggins was our "man of peace" who made a way for us in Southeast Denton. She agreed to come to our first service as our guest on her birthday. She even gave us a mayoral proclamation declaring April 7, 2007, "Bridge Church Day" in Denton!

We sent letters to pastors in town with an offering thanking them for their pioneering ministry in the city and assured them that we did not want their church people, we wanted to reach the lost and unchurched. God used two of those pastors to really encourage and bless us. Sadly, other pastors didn't champion our cause and opposed our creative efforts. In the light of opposing voices, those encouraging ones seemed like water on parched ground! We purposed in our hearts that some day we would champion and resource other churches. Where the devil tried to discourage us with criticism, God lit a fire in us to be cheerleaders for others.

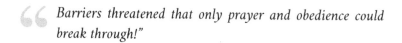

Barriers threatened that only prayer and obedience could break through!"

The week before the church launch, it felt like all hell was waging against us. Barriers threatened that only prayer and obedience could break through! People flew in from around the world to help us, but the weather forecast called for a record-breaking snowstorm. It hadn't snowed in April in North Texas in recorded history, but now the wintry mix threatened our outreach plans! Should we cancel? Would people come? In the midst of these questions, our son, Cody, fell on his scooter and broke both of his wrists.

A couple from Florida, Jody and C. J. Andrews, graciously relocated to help us plant. In the process, their identity was stolen and they engaged in the nightmare of trying to restore their accounts and dismiss false charges. Meanwhile, someone stole Kris's purse. Annoyances bombarded us on all sides, but we forged ahead with our plans. Rain, snow, or sleet, we were going to hunt Easter eggs and invite people to church! And that's what we did!

People came in the snow to hunt eggs, we made friends, gave away prizes, and invited people to come to church. God was doing so much more than you could see in the natural. God gave a dream of my wife to a sweet mom we call "Mrs. Maude." She brought her kids to the park and looked up to see my wife there—the woman in her dream! God told her to take her family to our church, and she has been a faithful pillar ever since. We even saw God save her husband in a powerful HUPER way!

That first Sunday, April 8, 2007, all of our prayers, finances, faith, friends, and family converged on the campus of Texas Women's University—the same place I had visited thirty-five years earlier to have my speech tested. My life had come full circle. I would stand on that property and proclaim the gospel with a message called "The Bridge to Beyond." Kris and I stood up on the fourth floor looking into the parking lot anticipating if anyone would come. A lifetime of maturing and a year of preparation came down to this divine appointment. The balloons were blown up, people were invited, the nursery was set up, the worship team was warmed up, the greeters were in place. Would anyone come? Suddenly, even with the snowy, cold weather, the cars began to pour in.

Both of our fathers came to support us as did two fathers in the faith, Dale Gentry and Brother B. C. Mullens. Brother Mullens, a childhood hero of mine, had served as my grandfather's associate pastor for sixteen years. I flew him and his daughter from Tennessee to see a best friend's grandson carry on with the work before he went to heaven. He was eighty years old and had never flown on an airplane before this. He said, "In all my decades in the ministry, I never got to help plant a church." He was on the prayer team and prayed for one of the people receiving Jesus that day. He went to heaven shortly after that.

Councilwoman Heggins brought us a welcome from the mayor and proclaimed April 8, 2007, "The Bridge Church Day." Our friend Martin Smith and the worship band, Delirious?, whose members we had met in England, agreed to play a song and do an interview. Two British sisters, Jackie and Caroline, saw on our Easter flyer that a British band was coming and wanted to hear an English accent. Kris greeted them and helped them fill out a guest card. They had no idea their life would never be the same—divine appointment!

I preached my heart out and as I gave the appeal at the end, twenty-seven people came forward to give their lives to Christ, including Jackie and Caroline. They found the bridge—to heaven! One of those people who received salvation that day was Sergio. His wife, Sita, showed him our flyer and said she wanted to come. I felt impressed to add their zip code at the last minute, and the Holy Spirit targeted it straight to them. Sergio resisted, but Sita insisted. He gave his life to Jesus that day and has never been the same! His whole family serves in The Bridge today. (We baptized them in the lazy river of our local waterpark!)

Many of those who received salvation that first day are still leaders in The Bridge. Even with the bad weather, four hundred twenty-seven people attended. Some were friends and family who came to help, but around three hundred were people from the community. HUPER! Beyond what we could ask or imagine. He will do it!

Monday morning, we were exhausted from the launch but glowed in the aftermath of all God had done. Then we got THE CALL. TWU called to inform us they would no longer honor our six-month contract. This was devastating because we had spent over $20,000 on advertising that location. How could we get the word out again? Professors complained about a church meeting on the campus. I think when they agreed to the contract they thought a small church with a handful of hymn singers would arrive. They weren't prepared for a large group of radical praisers.

We had the right to pursue legal measures to make them honor their contract, so we did seek counsel. And we prayed. The team agreed that a legal fight would distract us from our mission. We were not in the city to fight TWU. *We didn't come to sue people, we came to save people!* This was a battle with no spoils! We desired to be known in the city for what we were FOR, not what we were AGAINST! We bowed out and concentrated our efforts on finding another venue. I asked Danielle Vasquez to get on the phone and call every school, movie theatre, or hotel she could. Meeting rooms large enough to hold us were not easy to find or cheap to secure in Denton. We would need a HUPER miracle to break through this barrier!

Danielle found Strickland Middle School, which agreed to let us meet in their auditorium. We were thankful but had to readjust our thinking because it wasn't nearly as nice as our first venue. Picture a 1950s middle school with old wooden seats meant to fit middle school children. It wasn't ideal, but it was the open door! We set up kids' church in the music room, a nursery in the hallway, and prayer in the chemistry lab. We continued faithfully with the small ones at Strickland. One day I drove by the University of North Texas's performing arts building, the Murchison. Years before I had driven by it and felt God say our church would meet there one day. It seemed impossible. Another church had a contract there. How would we afford it anyway? . . . *Unless it was HUPER.* That day as I drove by, the Holy Spirit urged me to see if it was available. It was! The previous church had found another building. Time for us to JUMP again!

> *A breakthrough is a sudden, dramatic, and important discovery, development, or advancement that moves you through an obstacle or stalemate."*

Four hundred fifteen times, our amazing road crew set up and tore down for church with some of our best memories on the campus of UNT. Students would sneak out of their dorms to steal donuts, but some of them wandered in and were born again, and some are now amazing leaders. Who knew donuts could lead to salvation? After eight years and hundreds of hours looking at potential properties, we felt God say, "Rise and build." We didn't re-sign our office building lease we used during the week for meetings in faith that God was going to give us our own building. This left us with no place to meet during the week except for the living room of our intern house. It seemed like a temporary setback, but we believed it was for a great set up!

I stood up on January 2015 and announced to the church that we were going to see breakthrough this year in a building. I had no idea where or what it was, but I knew it was the *kairos* moment to believe. A few days later, I was driving down a road I didn't normally go down and saw a sign for some land. I called the number and an old man answered. He said, "Preacher, you don't want my land, but you might be interested in my church's property." Long story short, he introduced me to his pastor at Cooper Creek Baptist Church on Fishtrap Road. One hundred years ago, pioneer believers started a church there. Their little chapel can still be seen by the cemetery across the road. In 2001, they built a great new building on their five-acre property, but they had since dwindled to a handful of faithful saints. The aging church community needed to sell the property. HUPER story . . . within ten weeks from hearing about the property, we raised $350,000 for a down payment and moved in. HUPER breakthrough!

"Then I, God, will burst all confinements and lead them out into the
open. They'll follow their King. I will be out in front leading them."

(Mic. 2:13 MSG)

A breakthrough is a sudden, dramatic, and important discovery, development, or advancement that moves you through an obstacle or stalemate. In 2 Samuel we see where David and his armies defeated the Philistines at Baal-Perazim. David says, "As waters break out, the Lord has broken out against my enemies before me" (2 Samuel 5:20 NIV). David names the battlefield, Baal-Perazim, meaning "The Lord who Breaks Out".

Before you can *break through*, you've got to *go through*! Move out. Step into your divine appointment. Don't quit! What has God graced you to step through in this *kairos* season? No matter where you are, stir up the gift of God within you and see His power burst through the opposition according to His HUPER power working in you. The opportunity is definitely worth the opposition! You serve the "Lord of the Breakthrough," and soon your breakthrough will become someone else's—BREAKOUT!

11

THE HUPER HERO IN YOU: FIND YOUR PHONE BOOTH

> *In me is working a power stronger than every other power. The life that is in me is a thousand times bigger than I am outside."*
> —Smith Wigglesworth

THE WORLD WANTS SUPERHEROES. Marvel and DC characters seem to have a permanent place at the box office. There's a big difference between super and *huper* as it's lived out. I tried to be a SUPER-HUMAN to overcome my sin, defects, anger, and frustration. I mustered up all the inner superpowers I could and failed every time. God never asked us to be superhuman. Superman and Wonder Woman have their place in the comic book aisle, but the Bible never expected us to be super ourselves.

God knows our broken humanity, our weakness, and His purposed need for grace—beyond us! The Old Testament Law proved how we could not save ourselves no matter how SUPER we tried to be. God intended you to need something else and not be enough in yourself. Just as 2 Corinthians 12:9 (NIV) says, *"But he answered me, 'My grace is sufficient for you, for my power is made perfect in weakness.' Therefore I will boast all the more gladly about my weaknesses, so that Christ's power may rest on me."*

> *"My grace is always more than enough for you, and my power finds its full expression through your weakness."* So I will celebrate my weaknesses, for when I'm weak I sense more deeply the mighty power of Christ living in me. (2 Cor. 12:9 TPT)

We are earthen vessels created in His image but desperate for His presence to dwell in us. Huper takes us BEYOND our own limits and abilities into God's supernatural strength and power. BOOM! I think we just broke a barrier.

You're That Preacher Boy

I've talked a lot about my uncle John White and how God used him in my life. He's one of the best examples I've seen of God's HUPER power transforming someone beyond their limits. He contracted polio at two years old, wore a metal brace on his left leg, and dragged his right leg beside him. He should never have been able to ride horses and rope cattle, but he defied doctors and shocked his family. He worked harder than everyone else to prove he could compete with his brothers and impress his dad. His arms were like concrete pillars from lifting himself on and off horses all day. John determined to be defined by his strengths, not his weaknesses. He was a great example of how to be faithful with the very best we have. But, God had called him BEYOND himself.

When John was a boy, a traveling preacher looked at him and said, "You're that preacher boy." The minister saw past the SEEN

LIMITATIONS into the UNSEEN POSSIBILITIES because at that moment John didn't look like a preacher and for many years after that he didn't act like it. He knew the preacher's words were true, but John thought he'd continue living his own way; then one day his weakness finally caught up with him. He was married with two little girls when a steer turned on him unexpectedly, which resulted in him breaking his good leg. Now he had a brace on one leg and a cast on the other. He couldn't work, and he and his family had to move in with his mother in a small trailer house just behind the home I grew up in.

Humiliated and at rock bottom, God met Uncle John with grace at his most desperate place. Pastor Douglas, whom I mentioned in Chapter 2, visited him with an offering in a brown paper bag. John tried to run him off, but Pastor Douglas insisted and handed him the bag with over $800 in it. At first, John's pride and shame made him angry. He shouted, "Why would you do this?" Douglas answered, "Because God loves you, and so do we!" The truth of God's love began to break through John's stubbornness, and he and his wife began to experience miracles in the middle of their worst days.

Uncle John cautiously began attending church but wasn't sure about all the "Holy Spirit" stuff. One day we were returning from a team roping and John became so violently ill that he pulled over and made me take the wheel. I was fourteen with no driver's license and had never pulled a trailer more than around our horse lot behind the house. I had to drive the truck and trailer filled with horses while John lay on the floorboard of the truck moaning in severe pain. This frightened me because he was tougher than nails and never flinched at pain.

I knew Uncle John's condition was serious, so I started to passionately pray in the Spirit for healing. At first John resisted and told me to stop praying in that gibberish, but the more I prayed the better he got. When I stopped praying, his pain worsened, so he said, "Okay, keep praying!" After a while, he sat up completely healed and in awe at God's power. I said, "Why don't you go ahead and get filled with the Holy Spirit." He agreed and responded to the call of God on his life.

Uncle John longed to attend Bible school but didn't know how he could ever pay for it. Guess what? God had something up His sleeves. Someone dropped off money in another brown paper bag. (What is it with God using brown paper bags? I guess they're ordinary vessels.) It was stuffed with thousands of dollars, enough money for John to attend Calvary Cathedral Bible School in Fort Worth. That year gave him a foundation of God's Word, and he made his pulpit the arenas and his parishioners the cowboys he worked with. God took him beyond John's own determination into God's divine huper strength.

God told John, "You're that preacher boy." What does God see in you? Maybe He's even sent people your way to confirm it. You're that artist. You're that great Mom or Dad. You're that entrepreneur. You're that college graduate. You're that teacher who reaches the hardest cases. You're that missionary. You're that first responder. You're the first one in your family to overcome addiction. You can fill in the blank of God's prophetic potential over your life. Raise your hand and say, "Yes, I'm that overcomer!" We can give God our best, but how are these dreams and desires going to turn into reality? According to the HUPER power that works in us.

HE MAKES NOBODIES INTO SOMEBODIES

Philippians 3 presents the apostle Paul's impressive resume. He was the best stock of Israel, circumcised on the eighth day, of the tribe of Benjamin, a Hebrew of Hebrews, a Pharisee with great zeal, and blameless concerning the law (Phil. 3:5–6). These qualifications could have made him a Hebrew SUPERSTAR, but Paul said he counted them as dog poop! Then in 1 Corinthians he encourages, *"God has chosen the foolish things of the world to put to shame the wise, and God has chosen the weak things of the world to put to shame the things which are mighty"* (1 Cor. 1:27). I love how *The Passion* translates it . . .

He chose the lowly, the laughable in the world's eyes—nobodies—so that he would shame the somebodies. For he chose what is regarded as insignificant in order to supersede what is regarded as prominent, so that there would be no place for prideful boasting in God's presence. For it is not from man that we draw our life but from God as we are being joined to Jesus, the Anointed One. And now he is our God-given wisdom, our virtue, our holiness, and our redemption. And this fulfills what is written: If anyone boasts, let him only boast in all that the Lord has done! (1 Cor. 1:28–31 TPT)

The insignificant supersedes the prominent by God's power working through us. Our days of insecurity are over as we stop looking for ways to feel better about ourselves and shift our security to the unshakable, unbreakable confidence of Christ IN US, the hope of glory!

"Living within you is the Christ who floods you with the expectation of glory! This mystery of Christ, embedded within us, becomes a heavenly treasure chest of hope filled with the riches of glory for his people, and God wants everyone to know it!" (Col. 1:27 TPT)

We can give God our talents, our education, our accomplishments, our money . . . all we have to offer, realizing the same as the apostle Paul, it's nothing compared to HIM. Until we come to that realization, we'll continue in unfilled cycles of frustration. Our greatest attempts at being SUPER and boasts in our superpowers pale in comparison to his HUPER plan. That humility ushers in His amazing grace as we admit that without Him we're nothing but clay! In myself I'm just a man, but with the anointing of God on my life I become HUPERMAN!

BEYOND AMAZING

The minister John Newton penned the words to the hymn "Amazing Grace." We'd probably all agree that he'd qualify as a HUPER hero. What you might not know is that John was not always a minister. At one point he was a foul-mouthed, lewd slave trader with no moral compass whatsoever. In the middle of a terrible storm at sea, John remembered the words his mother prayed over him. All those seeds that seemed to be dead and of no effect in his life resurfaced and he cried out for God to save him. Years later he became an ordained minister, helped William Wilberforce end the slave trade in Britain, and wrote hundreds of hymns.

 I am not what I ought to be, I am not what I want to be, I am not what I hope to be in another world; but still I am not what I once used to be, and by the grace of God I am what I am."

— JOHN NEWTON

In Christ, John found a huper strength that he'd never known through the "amazing" grace of God. But as our Scripture in Romans 5:20 tells us, grace is not only *amazing* it is ABOUNDING, exceeding any joy or abundance we've ever known. Yes, the devil is bad and has done tremendous damage to mankind, but GOD is GREATER and His GRACE huper abounds! I reckon it is so! This brings us to other HUPER Scriptures that say how grace super abounds! It not only covers the debt, it brings us into abundant life.

> *"So then, the law was introduced into God's plan to bring the reality of human sinfulness out of hiding. And yet, wherever sin increased, there was more than enough of God's grace to triumph all the more!"* (Rom. 5:20 TPT)

That same grace John Newton wrote about is still at work today. *The Passion Translation* footnotes expound on Romans 5:20 saying, *"Paul speaks of God's grace in v. 17 as superabundant, but then adds the prefix, huper, making grace huperperisseuō, which could be translated super-hyperabundant grace! There is an endless fountain of grace that has been opened for us in Christ!"*[1] That grace causes us to not just overcome, but become "more than overcomers."

MORE THAN OVERCOMERS

Romans continues to make HUPER HEROS out of us. Romans 8:37 calls us not just conquerors but more than conquerors. The Greek phrase for "more than conquerors" is *"Hupernikeo,"* a compound word of "huper" (beyond) and "nikeo" (to overcome, to completely prevail). Nikeo is the same word that the famous shoe company with the motto "Just Do It" is named for. It's more than surviving; it's thriving beyond imagination.

> *"Yet in all these things we are more than conquerors through Him who loved us."* (Rom. 8:37)

Again, the phrase "more than conquerors" is "Hupernikeo."[2]
A compound word:

- Huper: beyond
- Nikeo: to overcome; to completely prevail

It's not just winning but running the score up on the enemy! It's like a football team is winning 55–0 and still playing their starters to "run the score up." God wants to use our lives to RUN UP the score for the kingdom of heaven against the enemy! Your victory in Christ is sure. Our enemy has been defeated and God ran the score up on the devil when He raised Christ from the dead and seated Him.

"Now thanks be to God who always leads us in triumph in Christ, and through us diffuses the fragrance of His knowledge in every place."
(2 Cor. 2:14)

We don't just overcome for us, but our victory and example of faith pioneers a path for someone else to follow. So we not only overcome, but my obedience helps others overcome! HUPER VICTORY! *Remember, favor is not just for us, but for all those who follow us. Walk in the FOG—the favor of God!*

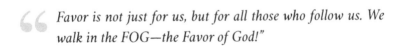

> *Favor is not just for us, but for all those who follow us. We walk in the FOG—the Favor of God!"*

This resonates with me so much because of my story. Born with a cleft lip and palate and never supposed to speak, yet God said, "I'll take that LESS THAN ordinary vessel and make him a prophetic voice to nations." He took a kid with a broken family and blessed him with a HUPER family. He took a boy whose family thought crossing the Red River was an overseas mission trip and sent him to every inhabitable continent, over fifty-five nations by his fiftieth birthday, and over 4.2 million air miles (that's almost seventeen trips around the earth). He took a boy who was too scared and insecure to even talk to girls and gave him a beautiful wife who is way out of his league (huper favor). I could go on and on to give God glory for what He's done through my weakness, but I think you get the idea. God is a BIG GOD who wants to do BIG things in our lives.

HUPER SIZE IT

Years ago in England, after I ordered a hamburger at McDonald's, the girl behind the counter asked me in a proper British accent, "Would you like to GO LARGE?" My mind tilted for a moment. *Go large?* "Oh, you mean supersize it!" YES! I wasn't sure what all that meant, but I agreed. "Yes, let's GO LARGE!"

Some of you may be thinking, *Duane, I know that. I've been in church my entire life! I know how BIG God is.* But, if we know it, why do we keep living so small?

*"Dear, dear Corinthians, I can't tell you how much I long for you to enter this wide-open, spacious life. We didn't fence you in. The smallness you feel comes from within you. **Your lives aren't small, but you're living them in a small way. . . .**"* (2 Cor. 6:11–13 MSG, emphasis added)

That smallness, I believe, often results from the tension between our ideological theology and our present reality. An invisible line exists between the SEEN and the UNSEEN—what we know in the WORD versus what we SEE in the natural! It takes faith to cross over the line and break the SEEN BARRIER into the promises of God. Huper is living larger than you can live on your own! Dream

BIG, and God will go beyond that—exceedingly, abundantly, and beyond.

Today, I'm behind the counter asking you, "Would you like to GO LARGE?" Or, better yet, "Would you like to HUPER-size your life?" Right now, take a moment to think about it. What area of your life do you desire God to take you BEYOND in . . . beyond your strength . . . beyond your ability . . . beyond your wisdom? Where would you like God's HUPER anointing to transform you? Reach out and ask Him. Move out in faith. Jump into your prayer closet, grab your X-ray vision glasses to see beyond the SEEN realm into God's UNSEEN possibilities! There is a GREATER you—empowered IN HIM! Let's find a phone booth.

 Good Enough = *the baseline living marked by mediocrity, being stuck in spiritual survival mode, and being controlled by complacency.*

Greater = *the life-altering understanding that God is ready to accomplish a kind of greatness in your life that is entirely out of human reach. . . Beyond what you see in yourself on your best day. But exactly what God has seen in you all along.* [3]

- STEVEN FURTICK, *SUN STAND STILL*

Find Your Phone Booth

No doubt you have heard of the American comic book hero Superman. Back in the 1950s, his adventures were put on television, and since then he has been portrayed in several major motion pictures.

Clark Kent, Superman's alter ego, was an epic nerd. He was a mild-mannered news reporter, but he wasn't a good reporter because he was never present when the story broke. I would have fired him. Stark differences existed between Clark and Superman.

- Clark wore ugly glasses. Superman had X-ray vision.
- Clark dressed very plain. Superman . . . well, you know, he had tights and a cape.
- Clark loved Lois Lane. He was always trying to get Lois to like him. But, he was way too average, too ordinary for Lois. She liked Superman, who always showed up when trouble arose.

Now, when trouble came, Clark seemed to disappear. Unknowingly, Clark was hunting for a phone booth. A transformation was about to happen! He came out of that phone booth, but instead of running away from trouble he headed straight for it. He asked, "Where is my phone booth? Give me just a minute. I'm going to change into another man—the real me—and when I get back, I'm going to face my trouble. I can change because I understand that I am not from this planet; I am from Krypton. Trouble, you cannot touch me!"

Superman was "faster than a speeding bullet, more powerful than a locomotive, able to leap tall buildings in a single bound." Is it a bird? No! Is it a plane? No! It's Superman!

You, like Clark Kent, may start out in life as a mild-mannered, average, ordinary person. The circumstances of your life may be trying to mold you into mediocrity. But today, if you understand who you are in Christ, you are NOT from this world—you belong to another kingdom, and you can step into your phone booth and be changed into another person. Instead of running from trouble, we look for a phone booth. We find a place of prayer and stir up the treasure within us!

Then the mantra of your life will be, "They are faster than any fiery darts of the wicked one. More powerful than any forces of darkness. Able to run through a troop and leap over a wall in a single bound."

"Is it a bird?" No!

"Is it a plane?" No!

"Who is it?" It's HUPERMAN!

God wants to do exceedingly, abundantly above and beyond your wildest dreams. If he did it for me, He will do it for you. He has huper anointing for you. He wants to take you beyond what is normal and reasonable and acceptable. He wants to take your life and make it so extravagant with His presence that only He can get the credit. God is an exceedingly, abundantly, and above God. From Genesis to Revelation and right on through today, He takes ordinary, normal people and uses them in exceedingly, abundantly, and above ways for His glory. You are called to a life beyond limits. Look for your phone booth, and let the transformation begin!

NOTES

PART I

1. Vine, W. E., Merrill F. Unger, William White, and W. E. Vine. 1985. *Vine's Complete Expository Dictionary of Old and New Testament Words*. Nashville: Nelson.

1. BREAKING BARRIERS

1. Bannister, Roger. *Four-Minute Mile*. Place of publication not identified: THE LYONS Press, 2018.
2. Corn, Joseph J. *Into the Blue: American Writing on Aviation and Spaceflight*. New York, NY: Library of America, 2011.

3. TREASURE EXPOSED

1. Sweet, Leonard I. *11 Indispensable Relationships You Can't Be Without*. Colorado Springs, CO: David C. Cook, 2012.

4. OUT OF THE BOX & INTO CHRIST

1. *Thayer's Greek Lexicon*, Electronic Database, Copyright © 2002, 2003, 2006, 2011 by Biblesoft, Inc. All rights reserved. Used by permission. BibleSoft.com

5. FACE THE FACTS, BUT EMBRACE THE TRUTH

1. Marr, Bernard. "How Much Data Do We Create Every Day? The Mind-Blowing Stats Everyone Should Read." *Forbes* magazine, May 21, 2018. www.forbes.com/sites/bernardmarr/2018/05/21/how-much-data-do-we-create-every-day-the-mind-blowing-stats-everyone-should-read/#532f9f7c60ba.
2. *Thayer's Greek Lexicon*, Electronic Database, Copyright © 2002, 2003, 2006, 2011 by Biblesoft, Inc. All rights reserved. Used by permission. BibleSoft.com
3. Ibid.
4. Ibid.

5. "BibleGateway." 2 Corinthians 10 TPT Bible Gateway. Accessed January 13, 2020. www.biblegateway.com/passage/?search=2+Corinthians+10+&version=TPT.

6. Jordan, Clarence. *Cotton Patch Gospels: The Complete Collection.* Macon, GA: Smyth & Helwys Pub., 2012.

6. BEYOND YOU

1. www.iona.uk.com/albums/detail/id/3/beyond-these-shores

2. *Paul McCartney's Liverpool Oratorio,* 1991

3. Jones, Howard O., and Edward Gilbreath. *Gospel Trailblazer: An African-American Preacher's Historic Journey Across Racial Lines: An Autobiography of Howard O. Jones.* Chicago: Moody Publishers, 2003.

4. "Dr. Martin Luther King, Jr. –1957 New York Crusade–The Billy Graham Library Blog." The Billy Graham Library, June 21, 2018. https://billygrahamlibrary.org/dr-martin-luther-king-jr-1957-new-york-crusade/.

5. "Crusade City Spotlight: New York, NY - The Billy Graham Library Blog." The Billy Graham Library, July 17, 2015. https://billygrahamlibrary.org/crusade-city-spotlight-new-york-ny/.

PART II

1. *Thayer's Greek Lexicon,* Electronic Database, Copyright © 2002, 2003, 2006, 2011 by Biblesoft, Inc. All rights reserved. Used by permission. BibleSoft.com

2. Ibid.

3. Ibid.

7. HUPER HOME: CONNECTION OVER PERFECTION

1. "BibleGateway." *Ephesians 3:14–19 TPT - Bible Gateway,* www.biblegateway.com/passage/?search=Ephesians+3:14–19&version=TPT#en-TPT-10572.

10. BREAKTHROUGH POWER: LAUNCHING THE BRIDGE

1. "G5550 - Chronos - Strong's Greek Lexicon (KJV)." *Blue Letter Bible,* www.blueletterbible.org/lang/lexicon/lexicon.cfm?strongs=G5550.

2. "G2540 - Kairos - Strong's Greek Lexicon (KJV)." *Blue Letter Bible,* www.blueletterbible.org/lang/lexicon/lexicon.cfm?Strongs=G2540&t=KJV.

3. *Thayer's Greek Lexicon,* Electronic Database, Copyright © 2002, 2003, 2006, 2011 by Biblesoft, Inc. All rights reserved. Used by permission. BibleSoft.com

11. THE HUPER HERO IN YOU: FIND YOUR PHONE BOOTH

1. "BibleGateway." *Bible Gateway*, www.biblegateway.com/passage/?search=Romans+5:20+&version=TPT.

2. *Thayer's Greek Lexicon*, Electronic Database, Copyright © 2002, 2003, 2006, 2011 by Biblesoft, Inc. All rights reserved. Used by permission. BibleSoft.com

3. Furtick, Steven. *Sun Stand Still: What Happens When You Dare to Ask God for the Impossible.* Multnomah Books, 2010.

ACKNOWLEDGMENTS

Many times in life God adds His HUPER to our life by the relationships surrounding and uplifting us. This has been my experience throughout the years displayed in many collaborations for Kingdom expression and advancement.

My wife, Kris, is the unseen mastermind behind this updated and expanded *Huperman* edition. She invested untold hours, putting her own projects on hold to retell my stories and display my life's mission in a fresh way. She deciphered decades of sermons, scribbles and sayings and prepared them into a hardy four-course meal. She's very good at setting tables and inviting people in to feed their hearts. When you read the pages of my journey—know that she's labored, loved and led along with me through thirty years of life and ministry. You can't really tell where I end and she begins; we are a team and this project is her labor of love.

Throughout the book I reference many people God has used to open doors around the world. Exceptional people like Bishop Tony Miller, Ralph Hagemeier, David Briggs, Stuart Bell, Jamie and Lea

Peters and those who have gone ahead of us like Rich Hubbard, Paul Godawa and Pastor B. B. Hankins. My life has been changed by National leaders like Bishop Thomas Muthee, Bishop Mark Kariuki, Raj Pata and Samuel Lamb who invited me into their nations and revealed Kingdom principles in exponential ways. I've been blessed with so many Kingdom connections around the world I could never name them all, but I honor the network of churches and believers God's connected me with to see HUPER things around the world.

A special thank you goes to Pastor Paul and Perrianne who enabled us to launch Beyond These Shores and have continued to cheer us on and inspire the journey. There are so many inspiring thoughts that originated in conversations with Perrianne, that I said, "Oh, I'm stealing that and running with it!" (I have given her credit a few times!) We truly know, "Not for ourselves were we born, but for the whole world!" Not many relationships span decades, and I'm thankful that ours has.

A special thank you goes to the *Beyond These Shores* partners who have sown and invested to share God's Word around the world. Thank you for believing in the vision BEYOND me. Only heaven will tell the full story of your harvest. These stories are your stories and every life touched and changed is your reward!

ABOUT THE AUTHOR

| Duane & Kris White

With the life anthem "Not for yourself were you born, but for the whole world," Pastor Duane White has traveled the globe preaching and teaching the promises of God. Born with a severe cleft lip and palate, Duane was told he would never be able to speak without impediment. Now he miraculously uses his "larger than life" communication style to challenge people to fulfill their extraordinary destiny. In 2000, he and his wife, Kris, founded

Beyond These Shores, which serves to equip, empower, and engage global leaders.

Duane has trained more than 125,000 leaders around the world, funded micro-business empowerment projects, equipped and resourced missionaries, and taken hundreds of people on short-term mission trips. Duane and Kris served with their family as missionaries to the UK for two years and have ministered in more than fifty-seven nations. In 2007, they launched The Bridge Church in Denton, Texas, a thriving local church endeavoring to connect "All Ages, All Races, and All Kinds" to life. Duane also leads the O2 Network of churches.

Duane has a Master of Ministry degree in Christian Leadership from Southwestern Christian University and has been in full-time ministry for more than thirty years. Duane and Kris have three grown children, Kelsey, Cody, and Ashton, and recently experienced the joy of becoming grandparents to Zion.

For more details and updates:
www.duanewhite.online
www.findthebridge.com
www.beyondtheseshores.com

facebook.com/huperduane
twitter.com/huperduane
instagram.com/huperduane

"HUPER THINGS" DOWNLOAD

Set your faith to music! Download the free "HUPER THINGS" song written by Anthony Fisher and performed by The Bridge worship team. It features a clip from Duane's iconic HUPER message from 15 years ago.

bit.ly/huperthings

Mɪɴᴅ Rᴇɴᴏᴠᴀᴛɪᴏɴ: 21 Dᴀʏs ᴏғ Tʜᴏᴜɢʜᴛ Tʀᴀɴsғᴏʀᴍᴀᴛɪᴏɴ

Would you like to renew the outdated thoughts devaluing your life? Your mind is prime property! Inevitably on home renovation shows, the homeowner must decide to recycle it, reuse it or repurpose it. The designer negotiates for the removal of tattered recliners, outdated appliances, and clashing wall colors. But change is scary, and it's hard to part with what's familiar and comfortable. "Don't worry! You will love it! It will be worth it," the professional encourages. "Just trust me." What if we could do the same thing with our minds? Would you like to demolish all of those negative thoughts and experience peace of mind? Thoughts direct our destiny and focus our future. Negative thinking deteriorates our life and invites anxiety to squat on the prime property of our mind. This is no DIY job—you need a professional! You can trust the Divine Designer to transform every thought into a remodeled reflection of the glorious "mind of Christ." Structured into three phases, this twenty-one day devotional provides you with the transformation tools required to renew your mind and change your life! Phase One, Demolition, tears down faulty belief systems and removes debris from the past. Phase Two, Foundation, rebuilds structures, daily habits and patterns of truth. Then the fun part—Phase Three, Interior Furnishings, adds a pop of color to array our thoughts with creativity and abundance. Are you ready? IT'S DEMO DAY! The original contractor is about to "flip" your mind, but He doesn't plan on selling—He's moving in to stay!

AVAILABLE ON AMAZON & KINDLE